Preemie Parents®

26 Ways to Grow with Your Premature Baby

TAMI C. GAINES

Foreword by Gaines M. Mimms, M.D.
Illustrated by Roni Orlina

SELLERS
PUBLISHING

Published by Sellers Publishing, Inc.

Written by Tami C. Gaines
Illustrations by Roni Orlina
Cover and interior design by Heather Zschock
Back cover photo and back flap photo © www.tonyturnerphotography.com

Sellers Publishing, Inc.
161 John Roberts Road, South Portland, Maine 04106
Visit our Web site: www.sellerspublishing.com • E-mail: rsp@rsvp.com

ISBN: 13: 978-1-4162-0630-9
Library of Congress Control Number: 2010933893

10 9 8 7 6 5 4 3 2 1

Printed and bound in China.

contents

Testimonials

"Tami Gaines…guides you through a place where no one wants to be, and leads you to a destination of hope, calm, and comfort. *Preemie Parents* is a must-read for anyone dealing with the journey between life and death."

— **Stephanie Brady,** *Mother of premature twins*

"In my thirty-one years of neonatal nursing practice, I have never seen anyone stop grieving the loss of their 'perfect' pregnancy and 'ideal' birth as quickly as Tami did. Any family who has experienced a premature birth should read *Preemie Parents* for its insights and to move through the experience with strength and a sense of peace."

— **Gail Lormand,** *Neonatal Intensive Care Nurse*

"Thank you for using your authenticity and honesty to share your journey and to teach and inspire us."

— **Julie G.,** *Mother of a premature baby*

"*Preemie Parents* will make you laugh, cry, and ultimately [it will] leave you feeling up-lifted and capable of conquering all of life's obstacles. Tami Gaines captures your heart and lifts your spirits from page one with her beautifully depicted journey through the life-changing experiences of marriage, motherhood, divorce, death, and especially life. With an open mind, a loving heart, and a positive outlook, Tami proves that anything is possible…even the seemingly impossible…This is a wonderful read for parents of premature babies, as well as for any member of the human race!"

— **Erin Marie Duffy,** *RN, MSN*

"I had a twenty-four-weeker, named Ali. I was given your book by the March of Dimes support person at Capital Health System, in Trenton, New Jersey. This was one of the most terrible experiences of my life and in your book I found much truth and inspiration in our shared experience."

— **Donna A.,** *Mother of a premature baby*

"The depth and perspective of *Preemie Parents* is powerful, in a situation that makes you feel so powerless. Thank you for your faith and determination."

— **Anonymous**

foreword

L ife begins with the first cry in the delivery room, but for premature babies, the journey starts when they enter the NICU. Although we do not know the course or outcome for the individual baby, every neonatologist awaits the predictable diseases and complications, based statistically on gestational age. We are limited in what we can prevent, but comfortable with the tools available to treat these infants. Parents enter dazed, overwhelmed by guilt and unspeakable fears for the future of their child. Many struggle with their own identity and loss of control while trying to learn how to parent their fragile child. Each week brings the bombardment of another medical hurdle to overcome and the introduction of yet another medical consultant to incorporate into the fabric of this strange, long journey.

Each story is intensely personal yet the shared experience is universal. Ms. Gaines tells a vivid and candid story of her family's experience in the NICU, while transforming her insights into powerful tools to help other families become advocates for these vulnerable infants. She challenges us as parents to look inside ourselves to find the strength, focus, and spiritual health to keep our child the priority at all times. She elevates the physician-parent relationship to a level that creates a powerful partnership that has but one goal: the well-being of a child. Over a career of twenty-five years, I have struggled to find the words that will help families during this journey. Ms. Gaines in *Preemie Parents* has achieved this by creating an emotional and spiritual framework for not only survival, but personal empowerment and transformation.

Gaines M. Mimms, M.D.

Acknowledgments

I would like to give thanks and honor to God and my universal messengers from whom I've received blessings, guidance, and limitless resources.

I would also like to thank the following earth angels who constantly walk with me, even when my path is uncertain…

My kids, Haili, Shane, Bria, and Trey, for their inspiration, energy and for giving me a sense of purpose.

Shandrea Gilchrist who flew 3,000 miles to sleep on a cot in my hospital room for five days so that I could manage the next five weeks; for running up huge phone bills so she could "check in" so that I wouldn't check out.

Camari Tomlin who continues to give me a clear and hilarious voice of reason in the middle of any and all madness, whether I want to hear it or not. I love you, cuz.

Nana Tomlin and Nana Gaines for giving me a foundation of faith, a framework for motherhood, and for passing to the next life to make room for the twins in this one. I am eternally grateful for your continued influence on my life.

For my parents and family for knowing when to step in, step out, and step up.

Ouida Vendryes for her spirit and faith and reminding me to embrace and honor the same.

Tanya Coke and Cheryl Marshall-Petricoff for taking good care of my kids while I was in the hospital on bed rest, so I could focus on taking good care of myself.

Ed Blunt for stepping confidently into the craziness of my life and giving me boundless support, wisdom, inspiration, friendship, and love. Thank you is simply not enough.

Sue Gilad, for having a vision of me that's so unbelievably large and unwavering, that I have no choice but to step into it for fear of letting her down.

Dr. Judy Banks for embracing my faith, for her daily communion with me while I was on bed rest, and for her ability to know when to speak from a place of friendship.

Gail Lormand for her sage wisdom and willingness to risk being reprimanded for doing the unthinkable, for my promise of keeping it unspoken, all in the name of the growth and development of the twins, their siblings, and their mom.

Dr. Gaines M. Mimms for his humanity, commitment, sense of purpose, and sense of humor.

Arlene McDonald for offering to be Trey's primary — primary nurse, primary cheerleader, primary information seeker, primary anything and everything.

Dr. David Cooper for unknowingly bringing calm to most storms and for helping my twins and me manage the simple act of breathing.

Felice Harrison for reminding me that the best education is not had in the classroom but rather while living life.

Tracy Nelson for showing up at exactly the right time, every time for the last nine years. The power of your friendship is matched only by the strength of your character.

Joeff Trimmingham, who has been the Captain of my dream team for the last two decades. Your faith, friendship, and calm have helped build the foundation of my success.

All of the neonatologists and sub-specialists at Morristown Memorial Hospital for believing, when they knew they probably shouldn't, in the sheer possibility of life.

Sibylle Preuschat for her connection with nature and her universal guidance.

Dr. Jsahna Simmons for making regular trips to the hospital to be sure I was well-nourished physically and mentally.

Everyone in my Market America family who ever sent out a prayer or good energy my way during my journey. I received them and appreciate every one of you.

The Rights Factory, my agents, and the all-star team at Sellers Publishing for their belief in the positive impact *Preemie Parents* could have on parents worldwide.

I've lost many brain cells in the last eighteen months. If I forgot anyone, it is without intention and I appreciate you.

Dedication

This book was written…

Under the bright light of my twins, Bria and Trey, born at twenty-five weeks. They are the smallest yet the mightiest teachers I have ever had.

I'm honored that they found our family worthy of their gifts.

This book was written…

In the shadows of my daughter, Haili, and son, Shane. I am so proud of these little people who stood tall and strong throughout our journey, on which they were unsuspecting participants.

My children's spirits drive me to be a better person each and every day.

This book was written…

With tremendous gratitude to my former husband, Bruce, for blessing me with our four angels.

This book is dedicated…

To the neonatologists and nurses who give hope.

To the families of premature babies who never lose hope.

To every premature baby that teaches us to always have

FAITH.

dear reader,

I am the mother of four children, the youngest of whom were twins born at twenty-five weeks. My journey was transformative and extraordinary in so many ways and common in so many more. I held on to several beliefs once the fog of being in the Neonatal Intensive Care Unit (NICU) cleared. I felt that the babies (not just mine but all babies) could pick up every energy vibration that presented itself in the NICU — good or bad. I believed that they had enough to deal with without reading the disconnected, stressed, and concerned energy of the adults who were supposed to be the stable ones. I also believed that one extraordinarily strong parent could set the tone for other strong parents, no matter how desperate the situation. My intention for this book is to share my coping mechanisms so that you, too, can be strong for your baby(ies), your family, and for *Preemie Parents*® everywhere. What I've described in this book is not the only way to make it through. I encourage you to take what you are able from the guidance provided here and mold it to suit your experience. It was only through the intersection of common sense, education, spirituality, and physical and mental fitness that I survived this all so well.

As you read my story, remember that you have a choice in how you write your own.

To your transformation,

Tami C. Gaines

Tami C. Gaines

from one preemie parent to another

If you want to become whole, let yourself be partial.
If you want to become straight, let yourself be crooked.
If you want to become full, let yourself be empty.
If you want to be reborn, let yourself die.
If you want to be given everything, give everything up.

— *Tao Te Ching* (Stephen Mitchell translation), Chapter 22

I'm assuming that you purchased this book with a sense of hope or expectation that within its pages you would find some explanation or rationale as to why your baby is in the Neonatal Intensive Care Unit (NICU). I know because when my journey in the NICU began, I did the same thing. I purchased every book that might provide a reason why this happened to our family or a way to make me feel better about the situation. I quickly realized that this experience is not about "why." It is about the "how" — how to cope with this unexpected reality; how to find joy in pain; how to find hope in the face of despair; and how to celebrate life in the face of death.

After reading the final page of the last book I'd ever purchase on premature babies, it became clear to me that there was too much information on the medical issues involved and not enough on the transformative aspects of prematurity. I had to be stripped down to my soul and rebuilt from the inside out so that I could receive the great gifts of my premature twins. And it is my intention to show others how to grow, as I did, through this experience.

At the outset, it was my intention to tell my story in a way that honors the NICU experience, provides the reader with a supportive embrace, and gives an umbrella of encouragement under which to walk during the NICU journey.

And what do I know of this journey? Unfortunately, quite a bit more than I ever would have imagined. You see, perhaps like you, I had no idea what to expect in the surreal world of the NICU I often stared in disbelief at my tiny twins and wondered how I would ever right myself from this experience. I felt lost, alone, and vulnerable among the alarms and ringing bells. I wasn't even sure if I should try and remember the nurses' names because I didn't know how permanent any of this was. I didn't know what to think, what to say, or how to act. The only thing I knew for certain was that I wanted my babies to live.

After three weeks of being in a state of shock, I realized that I, too, wanted to live. I did not want to feel sad or scared. I did not want to hesitate at the entrance of the NICU, weak with dread at the thought of what medical drama might wait inside. I wanted to stop replaying the images of frail, feeble sick babies that haunted my dreams and waking hours. They took a toll on my body, my mind, and caused distance between me and my other two healthy children.

It was also at three weeks that I held my son for the first time since his birth. I felt the strength of his heart and the grip of his tiny hand on my pinky finger. I knew then that it was time to travel this NICU journey with the intention of being an inspired mother whose power was only matched by that of my twins.

I had a clear picture of the person that I would need to become in order to provide the support, love, and protection that my babies (and all my children) needed in order to survive and thrive. I composed five simple Principles of P.E.A.C.E. that guided and influenced everything I did and thought…then and now.

Principles of **P.E.A.C.E.**

1. The **POWER** of intention is greater than any current reality.

2. Everything is **ENERGY**.

3. **ALL** things will move into balance eventually.

4. **CARING** for myself precedes caring for anyone else.

5. **EVERYTHING** is exactly as the Universe intended it to be.

THE POWER OF INTENTION IS GREATER THAN ANY CURRENT REALITY

Intention is an invisible force that gives power to whatever you want to create. Intention is one of the tools you can access to gain an emotional advantage over the NICU The concept of intention is explored more in the "U" section of *Preemie Parents*.

EVERYTHING IS ENERGY

Energy is a direct line from your body, mind, and spirit to the Universe. Everything and anything you think about manifests itself in some way… eventually. The Universe gives you whatever you say and focus on. It is critical to manage your energy — your thoughts, feelings, and speech — so that you can invite goodness into your life and the life of your baby.

ALL THINGS WILL MOVE INTO BALANCE EVENTUALLY

No matter how disconnected you might be feeling or the amount of discord in your life, all things will move into balance. Each element of your life will right itself because it is the natural order of things. If you remember this, you will be comforted by the knowledge that, eventually, harmony will prevail.

CARING FOR MYSELF PRECEDES CARING FOR ANYONE ELSE

Unless you are feeling whole and healthy, you will not be able to support your babies, your spouse, your children, or anyone who is relying on you for strength. The whole person includes your physical body, your mental body, your emotional body, and your spiritual body. Take time each day to nurture each of these "bodies" so that you can nurture others. This principle is further explored in the "I" section of *Preemie Parents.*

EVERYTHING IS EXACTLY AS THE UNIVERSE INTENDED IT TO BE
Rather than push against unwanted things (which ultimately causes you to focus on them, activating the Universe), fill your head with images of what you would like to have, to be, or to do. Once you fully accept your current situation without reservation, you will see opportunities for personal growth in every experience that you have, whether you judge it as good or bad.

These five simple principles are the underpinning of *Preemie Parents.* I used them to strengthen my beliefs that the Universe makes no mistakes, everything happens for a reason, and that there are always lessons to be learned. The principles of P.E.A.C.E. provide the framework for understanding how I transformed my NICU experience from one of great despair to one of extraordinary personal growth.

I was walking through the hospital parking lot on a glorious sunny day and I had a thought, as clear as the sky was cloudless. This thought literally stopped me in my tracks. I stared off into the distance as I heard the reality of my situation whispered in my ears. *These babies were not premature. They came exactly at the right time, for all of the right reasons, as was predestined for them by the Universe.* In fact, I was the one who was premature. I was not ready to redefine my life and expectations, to be jolted out of my comfort zone, to be made to face the realities of life and death, or to decipher trivia from importance. The bottom line is this: *We must redefine our beliefs about prematurity so that we can be entirely open to the opportunity for personal growth, embrace an enlightened life, and extend ourselves to our families without limits.*

As you read this book, I encourage you to experience it and to live its lessons. For when you do, you too will experience amazing transformation as you await your baby's homecoming. As we walk this journey together, I thank you for trusting me with your time and spirit.

my story

"Mom?" my young son, asked from the back seat of the car.

"Yes?"

"I want a little brother and a little sister."

I laughed out loud, "Shane, you have a better chance of getting a horse than getting a brother and sister. What color horse do you want?"

We picked up my daughter then and we all laughed as Shane retold the conversation we'd just had.

As it turned out, the horse was actually the long shot.

I shifted my position in my hospital bed for the tenth time, trying to get comfortable. I glanced at the clock quickly and then refocused on helping my five-year-old son, Shane, and my eight-year-old daughter, Haili, finish their homework before they had to leave. Just a few minutes before, I had called for the nurse and, in a quiet whisper, asked her to call my obstetrician. After four weeks on bed rest at the hospital, I knew "real" contractions from "uterine activity." These felt real and by this time I would know. I'd already experienced the full range of maternity experiences. My oldest was born on her due date in heroic fashion, after thirty hours in labor with no drugs and just five minutes before getting an emergency C-section. My second child was born at home, accidentally, delivered on the bathroom floor by my then-husband (who has no medical training). And now my twins were obviously about to be born, extremely premature.

Despite my best effort to focus on my kids, I couldn't help but think back to the events of my life that led me here. During a business trip at the end of October, I found myself inexplicably exhausted, unable to get up in the morning or stay awake past nine o'clock. I thought that I was overly stressed and vowed to start eating better and working out again. Several weeks later, I felt even worse and was convinced that I had something seriously wrong with me physically. Since I couldn't take any bad news in my already busy life, I decided to deal with it "later."

"Later" became four weeks. Laying in the tub, meditating on my failing health, I had an epiphany that led me to believe I was pregnant. The concept was nearly impossible, particularly since my husband had announced that we were officially done with babies and I'd reluctantly agreed to that. The next morning found me hiding in a bathroom taking a home pregnancy test. The two minutes that I waited for the lines to show up in the little window felt like two years…and, eventually, they appeared.

The next day, I mounted the stairs of my obstetrician's office and made the long walk down the corridor to verify what I already knew to be the case. It took her only a minute to confirm that I was indeed pregnant. She didn't miss a beat, when she added, "And it's definitely two." "What did you just say to me?" I shrieked. She just smiled and said, "It's twins." I almost fell off the table. I closed my eyes and said, "God has a great sense of humor."

I inherently knew that if I decided to keep these babies, my husband would leave me. It took me three days to tell him. He ranted and raved, threw things around the house, and stormed upstairs to call his best friend (and my worst nightmare) to commiserate about my purposeful pregnancy. My husband and I didn't speak for more than a day. Our next conversation was the day before my thirty-eighth birthday. He told me to terminate the pregnancy or he was leaving. I could see no reason to either terminate the pregnancy or stay with a man that would demand such a thing so that was that. My husband immediately "moved out" and up to our third-floor guest room and began living his single life. He came and went as he pleased, hanging out with his friends, and making it clear that his only interest was in finding a girlfriend and being away from me.

He ignored my growing belly, my fatigue, and my pleas for help and left me to manage my twin pregnancy, as well as our two older children.

During that time, I had no help. We had no babysitter or nanny and it was my responsibility to take the kids to and from school, oversee homework and school projects, and run them to their myriad of after-school activities.

The events from December to February remain a blur. I ran myself into the ground, shuttling the kids, contributing to school parties, running my business, preparing for the holidays, and dealing with the legal matters surrounding the separation. Shortly after Christmas 2005, God started calling family and friends back home. My maternal grandmother fell ill. Being the closest relative to her geographically, I arrived at the hospital first and sat by her bedside for more than a week with relatives coming and going before she finally passed.

Both of my grandmothers were tremendous role models for me. Nana Tomlin was a very accomplished woman and a wonderful spirit. However, her passing was a blessing to me, as she'd been living in a nursing home for more than ten years, stricken with Alzheimer's disease. The last few years of her life were not living at all. I spoke extemporaneously at her memorial service. With a swollen belly and thoughtful, calm voice that belied what was happening in my life, I told stories about my grandmother in front of the overcrowded room. I don't remember a word of my speech except for one piece. "My grandmother's favorite phrase was 'so much fuss over such a small thing,'" I said, my voice cracking with emotion. It's exactly what my Nana Tomlin would have said if she knew all that transpired over my happy, little pregnancy.

Shortly after Nana Tomlin's passing, I asked my brother, Derek, to drive with me to Hartford, Connecticut to see my last remaining grandparent, my other grandmother, Nana Gaines, who was in the hospital with kidney failure. She and I talked of tennis, politics, and my grandfather, who predeceased her. When my brother left the room for a few minutes, I told her of my twin pregnancy and impending divorce.

"He reminded me of your grandfather." She and my Pop were intensely in love and married for fifty-four years before he passed. "But I guess any nice gift wrap can make a package look better than it is." I nodded silently. "You've always been strong, Tami. Now you'll find out just how strong you really are. And I know neither of us will be disappointed."

On February 14th, Valentine's Day, we told our kids about our plans for separation. My husband used no tact with our young children and they both became inconsolably sad. His mean-spirited way of breaking the news to them, set me off and I railed at him. An hour later, I had my first contraction and I drove myself to the hospital to meet my doctor. I lay alone in the darkness, praying for the contractions to stop, and for my husband to move out of the house. It was all just simply too much for me to handle.

When I woke up the next morning, my contractions had stopped and my father was there (my sister-in-law had called him). He asked me if I wanted these twins. I told him I did and he went on to say that if I really wanted these babies to survive, I had to change the situation at home. I "had to do what I had to do" to remove my husband from the home. I told him I'd think about it. When I returned from the hospital, my husband was not there and, in fact, did not stumble in until 3:00 AM that morning, waking up the kids in the process. It was clear that he didn't care what happened to any of us. In the wee hours of the night, I signed the legal documents my Dad had referred to without so much as glancing at them.

A few days later, I was soaking in the tub and I felt the first baby "flutter" in my growing belly. That first kick was a jolt into reality. It was a kick that straightened my spine, righted my mind and, like the medical paddles that resuscitate a dying person, my heart jumped in my chest. I was back. And I was ready.

I soon realized that I could no longer maintain any semblance of what I was. I would have to close my ten-year-old consulting firm and focus on generating income that came with little effort on my part and provided time and financial freedom. I knew that I had to restructure my life to find greater balance between my professional aspirations and my personal priorities. Finally, I realized that I would have to quickly become extraordinarily self-sufficient, be mindful of my emotions, and fully embrace my new role as caregiver, provider, healer, friend, and chief cook and bottle washer for my kids.

I had to reestablish and reconnect with my most important relationships in a different way. Love took on an entirely new meaning for me. It became three-dimensional: self-love, love for my children, and love for their father. The last love was a lesson in forgiveness, understanding, empathy, and acceptance. When I was feeling at my worst physically and emotionally, so afraid and vulnerable, I dwelt on the fact that the man who was supposed to love me "for better or worse," had chosen only "for better." I blamed myself. I tried to figure out what I could have done differently.

I knew that I would not stave off the contractions if I wasn't good to myself. I made a commitment to myself to just be in each moment of my life and to not stress about the future or live in the past. With that, my spirit grew stronger, and so did my sense of motherhood, my priorities, and my belief that there was a reason for everything. Again, I remained pregnant.

On February 22nd, I went to the hospital for a routine ultrasound. I was watching my two little miracles on the screen, and glowing in the good news from the last few weeks: The amnio had come back negative for Down Syndrome. The detailed anatomy ultrasound had shown two healthy, thriving fetuses — a boy and a girl. And this ultrasound was going just as well. But wait. Why had the chatty technician fell silent as she stared intently at the screen? "I'll be right back," she said.

What now? I wondered. She came in with two other people but nobody said a word to me. I decided to wait this one out, humming quietly, willing everything to be all right. I just kept thinking, *I got the message, God. How much more could one woman take?* I glanced at the screen so I could see what they were seeing but I had no idea what I was looking at. Whatever it was, it wasn't good. As quickly as they came in, they left. The technician handed me a towel to wipe the gel off of my belly and told me, "Do not get up from the table. Someone will be right with you."

That someone was a nurse, who nearly carried me off the table and placed me gently in a wheelchair. I was immediately taken into an "observation" room, where they hooked me up to a fetal monitor and checked my vitals. When they were done, the on-call perinatologist came in and told me that I could not leave until they heard from my doctor. "What the heck is going on? I've been very patient waiting for someone to speak to me instead of about me." The doctor explained that my cervix was almost gone and I was having contractions. I asked if he was certain because I was not feeling anything and he simply picked up the charting paper from the monitor and showed me where the spikes represented contractions. They were everywhere. I finally broke down and had a really good cry. The kind of cry that makes you want to vomit. A cry that has so much pain and emotional exhaustion behind it that you feel like your heart is on the outside of your body for all to see, swollen and painful.

I did talk to my obstetrician and she said that I had to be admitted so I could rest and be monitored. I pleaded with her to let me go home and get my affairs in order and talk to my kids and then I'd come back. She gave me twenty-four hours to be back at the hospital.

Thankfully, my sister-in-law, Shandrea, was already on her way to my house from California for a "girl's weekend" with me. I told her everything when she arrived and she said, "OK. So let's think of this as a spa vacation." I rolled my eyes and she kept me company while I packed.

"What are you packing?"

"Like a week's worth of clothes."

"Tami, you're going to the hospital. Think hospital gowns. Why are you bringing all of those cute outfits?"

"Yeah, you're right." I stopped and began packing my laptop, files, books, and reports into another bag. She was staring at my blankly. "Well, I have to get some work done, don't I? What am I supposed to do, sit around in bed all day?"

The next morning, we hustled to get our nails done, and picked up snacks and a few items from the pharmacy. Our final stop was at White Castle for some really bad cheeseburgers. We laughed at the similarity to the scene in the movie *Goodfellas,* where Paulie (knowing he has to go to prison the next day) has a giant party with his family and friends, eats an enormous dinner, drinks great wine and, after he's sufficiently enjoyed himself, says, "Now take me to jail." In my mind, I was just going to a different kind of prison.

On February 23rd, I admitted myself to the hospital. I was twenty-one weeks' pregnant, fully effaced, 2 centimeters dilated, and in full labor. The perinatologist encouraged me to terminate the pregnancy as the fetuses wouldn't be viable at such an early stage. I refused because I knew at a cellular level that *these babies were a gift to me from God. Out of all the wombs in the world, they chose mine. I had to protect them at all costs and be open to the lessons that this experience would teach me.*

The perinatologist said that she'd have one of the neonatologists come and talk to me about the risks of having such premature babies and what our lives might be like if the babies were born now. "You know what?" I said as she rose, "I'm done talking to doctors. I don't want to hear any more of your bad news or the odds. It's enough already. I don't want to talk to any more doctors, nurses, specialists, or anyone who doesn't have something good to say."

She told me that she'd be really surprised if I was still pregnant in the morning and that she was just doing her job.

I said, "I know in my soul that these babies were meant to be here and I'm not giving up on them. And that's just me doing my job."

I watched the door close behind the doctor and turned to see my sister-in-law, Shandrea, smiling warmly at me. "You do what you gotta do. If you believe that you can stay pregnant, so do I."

I'd come too far and sacrificed too much to give up now. I was going to give my babies the best chance of survival that I could.

For the next hour, I laid in the bed, eyes closed, watching the colors dance behind my eyes, waiting for a sign, for information from the Universe to tell me what to do and how to do it. I could feel my shoulders relax and my body get heavy. Without warning, I got the sign — dates and words, which became the foundation of my statement of intention.

It is my intention to keep these two babies inside of my loving, protective womb until at least April 11th. Each Tuesday that passes, we will have a tremendous celebration of their growth and lives and the blessings they will bring. During this time of soulful reflection and calm, I will eat well, rest deeply, and laugh often. I love my children, both born and unborn, and will do anything I must to protect them. So be it. And so it is.

After my sister-in-law returned to California, I spent my days trying to arrange for friends to bring my kids to see me since my husband would not bring them. I tried to manage their busy schedules from my hospital bed. I had trouble sleeping because I missed them so much. The contractions began again.

I felt like I was always fighting. I was fighting to stop the contractions; fighting the dietary department for good food, delivered on schedule so I could gain weight; fighting the doctors who looked at me like I was crazy for trying; fighting loneliness; and fighting to feel normal — to be useful and productive — from my hospital bed.

I remember the day that I was just too tired to fight. I slept all day, waking only when they took my vitals or delivered my food tray. That night, I wrote in my journal until my eyes grew heavy. The next morning, I awoke early. It was snowing outside of my small window and I felt very quiet. I'd stopped pushing against my reality. A peaceful calm began to settle over me and I spent less and less time fighting against what was happening and more and more time on building up myself.

A nurse coming to take my vitals shook me back into my present situation. I looked at the clock silently willing my friend to come and grab my kids before I was wheeled down to Labor & Delivery. My goal was to keep the twins in my belly until April 11th at which point they would be at twenty-eight weeks' gestation and would have a fighting chance of survival. Unfortunately, it was March 14th and staying pregnant any longer didn't look likely.

I remembered that peaceful feeling and tried to recapture it in the midst of my strengthening contractions but I just could not get there. Again, I looked at the clock. Where was my friend to pick up Haili and Shane? Suddenly, there was a flurry of activity in my room as my obstetrician came in. One of the nurses took my kids down to the nursery to look at the newborns while Dr. Banks checked me. She doesn't have a poker face, so I knew: This was it. She quickly gave orders to the remaining nurses and residents and they made preparations to move me from the Anti-Partum unit to Labor and Delivery. I felt an IV being inserted in my arm and a warmth spreading across my chest as they began to administer magnesium to stop the contractions.

When my friend showed up to take my kids, I hugged and kissed my children goodbye and told them to have a great day at school. I could hear the elevator doors close and seconds later, I was transferred to a labor bed and wheeled quickly down the hallway. Within minutes, the room was full of nurses, doctors, anesthesiologists, and residents.

Thirty minutes later, my contractions had slowed and I was feeling very loopy from the magnesium. For twenty minutes, everyone waited for the decision to be made on whether or not to deliver the babies. But, while my mind was cloudy my voice remained clear — I would not consent to delivering them until they were really ready to come on their own. People began to leave reluctantly until the room was empty except for my doctor. "The neonatologist has to come talk to you. These babies could be delivered any minute and you should know what you're up against."

The neonatologist was devoid of emotion as he told me that at twenty-four weeks, the babies were right on the edge of viability. He wasn't very encouraging; in fact, he was downright pessimistic. He droned on and on about the likelihood of birth defects, chronic health issues, and the general uncertainty of the long-term prognosis. He also mentioned that the best thing for all parties might be to terminate the pregnancy. When he left, I said to no one in particular, "He has no idea who I am. And he hasn't met my babies yet."

Yet and still, I had to make a decision regarding the twins. The doctors wanted to know, under what circumstances would I authorize the doctors to "save" the twins or to let them go? I decided to leave it up to God. I instructed the doctor that he and his team should take their cue from the twins — if the they came out kicking and screaming, the medical staff were to do their best doctoring and apply their most heroic efforts to help them live. If they looked and acted like their souls were reluctant, I'd let them go with blessings and gratitude, for even their existence in my womb had changed my life. "You'd better bring your 'A' game, doctor," I said from my magnesium haze. "If you haven't seen it in awhile, you better go dig it up. I know these babies want to live."

I made it through the night, still pregnant to everyone's amazement. Under no circumstance was I allowed to get out of bed or even sit up. I used a bedpan, ate and drank lying sideways, was given sponge baths, and spent the majority of my time lying on the bed upside down, hoping that sheer gravity would keep the babies inside of me. I began to have trouble breathing and became very congested from being upside down. They put me on oxygen support and still I fought on. I could feel my once-muscular body weakening. Ignoring the physical pain, I kept the babies inside for another week.

On Monday, March 20, 2006, I got a raging fever and a blood infection that ravaged my body, taking the last of my physical strength. I dozed intermittently that night, sensing even in my fever-induced sleep that I was about to come face-to-face with my destiny — and that every bit of self-truth that I'd tried to avoid for the last thirty-eight years was bearing down on me. When I awoke early the next morning, the room was full of doctors, nurses, and technicians gowned and ready for action. It was another Tuesday, March 21st. I was twenty-five weeks' pregnant and this did not look like much of a celebration. I looked at my doctor and said, "Did I miss the party?" She told me that she was "throwing in the towel. Tami you've had a fever of 104° for most of the night and we have to get the babies out of the soup as soon as possible. This is dangerous for all three of you."

Nine months seemed so far away
to wait for these miracles to come our way
Our new twins must have felt this way too
because they arrived much earlier than they were due!

Haili and Shane proudly announce
the arrival of their sister and brother...

Bria Camari & Trey Bourne

March 21, 2006

10:48 a.m.   10:50 a.m.
1 pound, 12 ounces   1 pound, 13 ounces
12.5 inches   12.2 inches

Proud Parents: Bruce & Tami Nelson

Please think of us as we anticipate a joyful homecoming for our precious ones

Bria   Trey

"No!" I yelled, "I can do it! I can keep them in." The last word trailed me as an echo in the corridor as they whisked me away to the operating room. I received a spinal epidural and I remember very little after that.

The next night, I awoke to the feeling that someone was in the room with me and assumed it was a nurse but no one came into view. I waited and said, "Hello?" tentatively. Still nothing. I turned to look out of the window and out of my peripheral vision I saw a faint image of a large, red hat. Just like the kind my Nana Gaines wore. I started crying then and talking to the empty room about how afraid I was that my babies would die; and how afraid I was of being so sick, and that I would give my life at that very moment for theirs. The hat became clearer just for a moment and a whisper in the darkness said, "Let it go."

"I don't want to let them go!" I almost yelled. "I want them to live."

"Let it go," the invisible, soothing voice said again. The second time, I really heard the voice — "let it go" not "let them go". Another whispered "let it go" and I did. I let it all go that night. I was done with it all. I fell into the most peaceful sleep I'd had in months and woke the next morning to the hospital phone ringing.

"Hello?"

"Tami. It's me, Daryl." It was my brother calling from Baltimore.

"How are you doing?"

"I don't know. I haven't seen the doctor yet today."

He laughed a bit, "All things considered, right?"

"What do you mean?"

"Nobody told you?"

"Told me what?" I just heard a groan from the other end of the phone. "Daryl, did Nana Gaines die?"

"Yes. She died last night. I'm so sorry. I thought someone would have told you."

"They didn't need to. She was here last night."

Daryl said quietly, "You sound tired. I'll let you go."

I was very sick for the next several days and couldn't visit the babies in the neonatal unit. When they finally wheeled me to the NICU to meet Bria and Trey for the first time (again), I wasn't very coherent. I fought through the fog of antibiotics, painkillers, and Ambien to try and focus on my little babies.

"Why are they under the sunlights? They're black. They hardly need a tan." I heard a few nervous laughs.

"What's in their nose?"

I was told, "They are on ventilators because their lungs are underdeveloped. It's how they breathe."

"They're so small. How much did they weigh?" I asked. The nurses cut their eyes at each other. I'd obviously been given this information before but couldn't remember.

"One pound, twelve ounces and one pound, thirteen ounces."

"What?" I said. "I order more deli meat than that at the grocery store." There was more nervous laughter.

I looked at the nurses and the babies and said to no one in particular, "They will live. They will be fine."

I'll never forget the silence that followed for as long as I live.

"They will live," I said again with more conviction. And then I asked to go back to my room so I could sleep.

The babies first three weeks in the NICU proved to be indicative of the emotional roller coaster that was to follow. My son, Trey, died several times and was calmly brought back to life as if this were the natural order of things. Both babies fought infections that required the intervention of infectious disease doctors. Unexpectedly and joyously, their brain ultrasounds were normal — no IVH. They were both found to have heart murmurs. Blood transfusions were common. Apnea and bradycardia were regular occurrences. Trey was taken off of the ventilator and put back on several times during that first month. Little did we know that he would not breathe again without mechanical help for the foreseeable future.

My journal entries in those early days were lots of statistics and medical information. The following passage was one of many in which I tried to put my feelings into words:

> When I speak with truth and act from love, I am one with the messenger of life, the force that brings forth buds from trees and creates stirring and growth everywhere on the planet. I have the power to give the twins everything they need to survive. I must remember to find the giggle in the empty room.

THE 26 WAYS TO GROW WITH YOUR PREMATURE BABY

Before you turn to the "26 Ways to Grow with your Premature Baby" section, please remember that these are strategies that I used to grow through my NICU experience. Your circumstances, personality, and values are likely different than mine are. Because of that, all 26 ways may not resonate with you and that's all right. Take what you feel makes sense for you and your family and leave the rest. In fact, develop your own survival strategies and share them with us on our Web site — www.preemieparents.com!

I call these "little ways" because they are very much like your little baby(ies). My survival strategies are little things that will have a big impact on your NICU journey. Your little baby(ies) will also have a big impact on your life.

The "ways" that are presented in the next section are alphabetical, with each letter representing one survival strategy. I suggest reading this section through once in its entirety and then re-reading those sections that address challenges that you are facing immediately — perhaps it's your relationship with your baby's doctors or how your family has been treating you — really focus on those chapters that will help you right now and put those "ways" into action first.

As you read this section, you will notice some boxes labeled "Tami Time." These are real stories from my own experience with my twins in the NICU. Other boxes have an icon of a present on them. These are my gifts to you: additional resources to help you better navigate your journey. I encourage you to visit www.preemieparents.com for ongoing support and to become part of the larger community of courageous and loving *Preemie Parents*.

26 Ways

to grow with your premature baby

A: Advocate

It is no accident that "advocate" is the first of our NICU survival strategies. It is the most important concept during your NICU experience. What does it mean to advocate? The dictionary definition says: "to speak, plead or argue in favor of." As a parent or caregiver of a NICU baby, advocating is your single most important role — not parenting. In fact, technically, you are not the guardian of your child(ren) while they are in the NICU (just ask the Social Security Administration); the hospital is!

I n the world of ringing bells, alarms, and sick babies, at first it may seem that advocating for your baby is impossible and unimportant — especially because the majority of us have no medical training. Advocating in the purest sense of the world is speaking on behalf of someone else, typically someone who cannot speak for themselves — in this case, your child.

WHY DO I NEED TO ADVOCATE? I TRUST THE DOCTORS.

While your baby's caregivers are highly skilled and qualified, they are not staring at your baby day in and day out, watching his every move, hanging on her every breath. In many cases, you will know before they do that something just "isn't right." You will have an instinctual sense for what is right for your child. Do not ignore what you know to be the case just because you can't package it in medical terms. The hierarchy of knowledge about your baby is as follows:

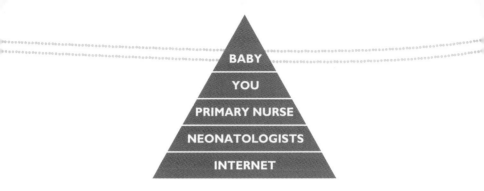

At the top of the pyramid is the baby herself. Every baby knows innately what is in his best interest. It is part of their spiritual knowledge and if they could speak or write instructions, they'd probably get out of the NICU much faster! Following closely behind the baby is you. Your reality is staring at your baby for hours on end. Your sense of what is right and wrong with your baby's care is stronger than you can imagine. When you acknowledge and embrace this fact, you become a powerful advocate.

Your baby's nurse (primary or someone with familiarity) is the next line of defense. He/She is with your baby even more than you are. And his/her experience is bolstered by years (sometimes decades) of experience. At times, your role as advocate will be to remind the nurse of the subtleties of your child. For example, does he like to be swaddled? Does she like her pacifier? Do loud noises bother him? Respectfully remind the nurse of the little things that will make your baby(ies) happier.

The neonatologists stabilize the pyramid. In some cases, they have been saving little lives for longer than the parents have been alive. While all "neos" have the best interests of the baby in mind, depending on their focus (nutrition, breathing, development, etc.), they may tend to make decisions without taking your baby's "big picture" into account.

TAMI TIME

Whenever I had a conversation with a neonatologist about the health of my babies, I always asked the nurse to join us. This serves three purposes: (1) it brings the nurse into the care plan firsthand; (2) the nurse becomes an interpreter for you as you ponder the conversation; and (3) during particularly emotional conversations, the nurse is a second set of ears and can remind you of points you may have missed.

Respectfully remind them, for example, that while nursing may fatigue your baby in the short run, it's developmentally appropriate and should not be ruled out.

The last rung on the pyramid is the Internet. While the Internet has made consumers smarter, in the world of the NICU it is dangerous if not used properly. Web sites related to preemies are published by parents, educational institutions, hospitals, doctors, nurses, religious icons, for-profit businesses, not-for-profit businesses, and even the government. With such a wealth of information from different sources, it is critical to be aware of the sources of information and the author's ultimate motivation. In addition, every baby is different and a tale told by one parent online is certainly not the only approach or outcome. You will drive yourself crazy gathering information from unreliable sources and then running into the NICU to share what you learned with your baby's doctors and nurses. The best way to use the Internet is as a research source after a discussion with a doctor or a nurse to better understand a health concern.

Speak with confidence on behalf of your child because she can't speak for herself. The goal is to be sure that *everyone is acting in the highest good of the baby.* Advocating is not a power struggle nor is it an opportunity to feed egos. Advocating is a respect-based, rational conversation between adults that results in an advancement of the baby's health, growth, and development — one that leads to a healthier baby who's able to come home sooner.

THAT SOUNDS GREAT. HOW IN THE WORLD DO I DO THAT?
In order to be a successful advocate, you have to be impossibly objective and unemotional when assessing the status of your baby. As a parent, you are emotional, stressed, distracted, angry, sad, confused, helpless, and happy (did I miss any?). Every emotion you feel as a parent of a NICU baby is justified and should be acknowledged. However, as an advocate, you must embrace those emotions and put them in a box so that you can listen clearly, process fully, and ask the right questions. Be thoughtful, reflective, and patient. If you don't understand something, ask for clarification. If you still don't understand something, ask again or ask someone else.

Steps to Becoming a Strong Advocate for Your Baby

1. **Remember that your baby's life is on the line.** It is that serious.

2. **Information must be gathered before opinions are rendered.**

3. **Your baby is different from his/her neighbor.**

4. **Pick your battles.** Everything is not equally important.

5. **Fall on your sword for that which you care about most deeply.** This is worth expanding on. My obsession was with my babies' nutrition and development. During every conversation, including those around surgery, I wanted to know when they would start feeding the babies again and how the procedure would affect them developmentally. Pick a "theme" (feeding, nutrition, breathing, development, long-term health) and stick with it. You can't be an expert in everything.

6. **Be an excellent student of the NICU** but remember that you are not a teacher.

7. **Choose the right time to advocate.** Never during the doctor's "rounds," in a crowd, or during a casual conversation in the hallway.

8. **Find a champion to support your cause** (another neonatologist or a nurse, for example. Never another parent!).

9. **Go out of your way** to be sure that all key players are on the same page (doctor, nurse, therapist, nutritionist, spouse, etc.).

10. **Know when to say "when."** Always remember that you are on the same team as the doctors and nurses. When advocating for a particular issue, it is a battle fought in the larger war. The war is won when your baby is home. Losing a few battles will not change the definition of victory.

11. **Thank the loser.** Give them another chance to help you with something else.

B: Be Present

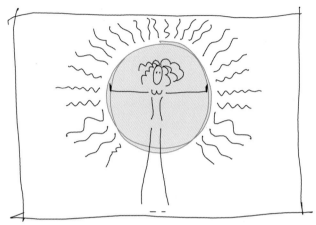

*Be present. Let your body and mind be
where they are physically right now.*

Do not allow your mind to wander. Do not spend what little energy you have pondering "what ifs." Do not allow anyone or anything to take you from the place you are right now. Experience every minute fully. Every ringing alarm, every small step forward, each conversation, every emotion…it is these specific moments that make up minutes, that make up hours, that make up days, that make up weeks, that make up months. Live in the moment and the rest will follow. When your life is lived in the moment, you will cherish it so much more than if it is lived in the past ("Why did this happen?") or in the future ("When will my baby go home?").

When you live your life presently, you acknowledge that everything is exactly as it should be. You reaffirm your faith that there is a Higher Power guiding us all and that the Universe does not make mistakes. If you trust that where you are is exactly where you are supposed to be, you will bring yourself, your baby, and your family Peace.

Steps to Being Present

1. Practice. When you are grocery shopping, listen to the hustle and bustle of the people around you. Smell the sweetness of the produce and the pungency of the seafood. Feel the crispness of the dollars in your hand as you pay.

2. Meditate. This does not require formal training or an instructor. All you have to do is be quiet – quiet your mind for 10 minutes a day so that you can be fully present for the remainder of the day. A beginner's guide for meditation follows on the next page.

3. Remove all negative distractions from your life — anything that takes you to the future or into the past. Avoid arguments and confrontations. If you hate your job, now is the time to take time off.

4. Make your life simple. If the thought of cleaning your house gives you anxiety, hire someone to do it (even if only temporarily). Better yet, when someone asks if you need help with something, ask him or her to come over and do a load of laundry.

5. Train yourself to recognize the times when you are not being present and then immediately bring yourself back to this very minute again.

TAMI TIME

Before the twins, my car was my mobile office. Afterwards, I limited cell phone calls to critical ones only, turned the radio off, and always cracked the window for fresh air (rather than the hospital's recycled air). It was just me and the scenery, noticing things in the landscape that had previously escaped me and just enjoying the solitude of the drive.

QUIETING YOUR MIND USING BASIC MEDITATION

There are literally dozens of ways to settle your mind so you can be in touch with your soul. Here, I offer a few of the processes that I used while in the NICU.

It is important to quiet your mind daily so that you can become inwardly strong to help you deal with the hard moments that you will encounter in the NICU. Your inner strength is your immune system that will protect you against the parasites and negativity of the NICU and all of the powerful emotions that come along with it. When you find quiet time, your mind can reflect on your journey and recommit with real intent. Every time you find peace within yourself, you inoculate yourself again so you can handle setbacks and disappointments and appreciate the victories.

In general, your goals of being quiet are to: (1) withdraw from active involvement in life for a few moments; (2) concentrate, which leads to contemplation; (3) reach a realization or recognition of a connection with your soul, the Universe, or some other Higher Power.

1. Sit in a comfortable position upright, with your back and head straight. This could be in the breastfeeding room, your car, on the grass outside of the hospital…literally anywhere where there is very little noise.

2. Warm up by closing your eyes. Breathe through your nose. Focus on your breath — cool air in, warm air out. If the mind wanders, gently bring it back to the breath.

3. Then examine your body from inside. How does it look? How do you perceive the inside? Where are the organs? What color are they? What is their condition — healthy, sick, tired, full of life? Slowly, step by step direct your attention to all the major parts of your body, start down, finish up.

4. With an imaginary broom, sweep out the tension and fatigue starting at the bottom with your feet and finishing on top with

your head and then gradually, gradually let a feeling of pleasant relaxation enter your body, as if a vast seascape has opened up before you.

5. Open your eyes and concentrate intently on a single object until all thoughts vanish from your mind, except an intense awareness of that object.

6. Allow all the sounds, thoughts, perceptions, and emotions to enter. DO NOT JUDGE OR ANALYZE THEM. Let these inner and outer happenings have a place inside you but do not dwell on them. Let them begin and end of their own accord, without your participation.

Don't worry about how you are doing. This is your process and you will practice quieting your mind in a way that works for you.

After your mediation, it is sometimes helpful to repeat an affirmation. You can make up your own or use one of mine:

- "I am grateful for being here. I recognize the value and power of this time. I feel very good being here."

- "God will only give me what He/She knows I can handle. I can handle this."

- "This is only a point in time. This too shall pass. There will come a time when I am relaxing on a beach with my family around me, marveling at nature's glory."

- "I accept where I am and welcome the insights I am gaining."

- "I have faith in my ability to manifest what I want and to set loving intentions to achieve it."

- "I choose to live with a sense of excitement and possibility about all the uncertainty in my life."

C: Calendars

Calendars. Put them in a drawer.

Keeping a calendar of appointments and scheduling future engagements is not only impractical, it takes you away from being present. Life in the NICU is unpredictable. There's little you can do to change that. My twins were born on March 21st. I made a dinner appointment with a colleague for April 28th. We rescheduled time and time again because of something that happened in the NICU that I felt I needed to be present for. Today is October 4th, and we still haven't had that dinner. Rather than getting stressed about canceling time and again, I finally realized that scheduling anything more than a few days in advance will cause stress. I can remember an appointment that's going to happen in a day or so in my head.

Put your calendar away. Turn your iPhone off. Take the battery out of your Blackberry. Learn to live life in the moment. Be spontaneous with your plans to go out. When someone invites you to a party, respond, "Based on all I have going on, going to your party will be a game-day decision." If that's a problem for the host, simply decline the invitation. There will be other parties. There will be other opportunities to go to dinner. There will always be another chance to do whatever it is you are trying to do.

Steps to Living without Your Calendar

1. **Remember that your NICU experience will end one day.** You can live life by a schedule after that.

2. **Don't let someone else keep your calendar after you've made a decision to live without it.** When someone used to ask me, "When are the twins coming home?" I'd simply say, "I don't ask those questions because it doesn't matter. All that matters is that they come home one day." The person usually gets very quiet and never asks again.

3. **Don't be pressured** into planning too far into the future.

4. **Replace your calendar with a journal.** Record your feelings and emotions, and chart your baby's progress in a positive way.

5. **If you must have a calendar,** choose one that only shows you today's date, rather than a week-at-a-glance or a monthly calendar.

TAMI TIME

I knew from the first meeting with the doctors that I'd need a really organized system for tracking information, emotions, and thoughts. The external information was too much not to write down for reference. My emotions came too fast and changed too often to simply let them go. It wasn't about a calendar though. It was more about comprehensive journaling.

D: Doctors, Residents, Nurses

For much of the time, your baby's doctors, residents, and nurses seem like God. They are the bearers of good news and bad; hope and despair. They hold, in their hands, the knowledge of your baby's future — the next surgery date, the move from isolette to open crib, the discharge date. Bless them for they are, in fact, only human.

You will see them more frequently than you see your best friend. The doctors, residents, and nurses that take care of your child will often be the most important people you connect with daily. They will give you the good news and bad; the best-case and worst-case scenarios; the statistics and the research; the shrug of the shoulders when they are baffled. It is easy to misdirect emotions at your child's caregivers as your frustration grows.

I encourage you to remember that your baby's healthcare providers are only human. They have feelings, families, and emotions. While they do the best they can, they are in fact, not too different from you. I remember when I became clear that this was the case.

For the third time in his short life, the doctors attempted to take my son, Trey, off of the ventilator and move him to continuous positive airway pressure (CPAP). The extubation went well but it was clear after just a few minutes that Trey was not ready for the reduced oxygen support. The doctors and nurses asked me to leave so they could reintubate Trey. As I'd done before, I went to wait on a bench just outside of the entrance to the NICU and could feel my anxiety grow as five minutes became fifteen and then thirty-five. I knew this process to take only a few minutes. Suddenly, there was a rush of nurses and additional doctors running toward Trey's crib. I couldn't see what was happening because Trey's area was screened off. One of the neonatologists ran out of the unit to make a call and I grabbed her, "What's going on? Please tell me." She looked at me sympathetically and said, "We're having some difficulty getting Trey reintubated. We need help and he only has a few minutes." She disappeared behind the desk and the next thing I heard was, "Dr. Jacir to the NICU stat. Dr. Jacir to the NICU stat. Anesthesiologist to the NICU stat. Pediatric anesthesiologist to the NICU stat." And then the hospital sister came to pray with me. I allowed her to sit with me but I was deep in a conversation with God — promising Him nothing but asking of Him. . .the world.

About ten minutes later, a parade of medical experts, nurses, and support people left the NICU looking drained, exhausted, and basically spent. Dr. Mimms was the last to leave. He said to me, "Why don't you go in and see Trey and then we'll talk." I ran to Trey, tears streaming down my face as I held his face in my hands and told him for the thousandth time how much I loved him and how much we wanted him to stay with us. He was in a deep, drug-induced sleep and didn't respond but I talked until I'd said it all. It was only then that I followed Dr. Mimms into the conference room.

He thought for awhile before he spoke and then he said, "We must find a way to keep Trey safe."

I looked at him a bit confused.

Dr. Mimms said, "We can't help him get better if he's not safe. He is too big to have a tube down his nose. Unless someone is sitting right at his bedside, we have to keep his hands bound to prevent him from pulling the tube out. That tube is the only thing that stands between life and death for Trey."

"OK, so we'll keep his hands bound," I said.

Dr. Mimms looked down and said quietly, "He's just not safe. He needs to have a tracheostomy."

"What are you talking about?" I said firmly and felt my emotions beginning to rise. "Do your job and he'll be safe. He's fine and you just need to tell the nurses to be more careful about watching him."

"Tami, we almost lost Trey today. He almost died. Do you understand that?"

"But he didn't die. He's still here," I said

"Tami, all I could think was that I would have to come in here, look you in the eye, and tell you that we did all we could but we lost him. Your son was dead. I can't bear the thought of that. I love Trey." And with that, his face got very red and his eyes filled, and his hands shook slightly as he reached for his yellow legal pad — that damn pad. It was the one he used to illustrate whatever procedure they were going to do on Trey.

It was the first time I'd ever seen a doctor, in any circumstance, become emotional about a patient. He did love Trey and I loved him for it. Having a hole cut in Trey's throat, into which a contraption would be inserted, was almost too much to bear. I began to shake my head no — both from disbelief and from the reality that another one of my perceptions of "normal" was to be shattered. I started to speak again and then I looked at Dr. Mimms, barely holding it together. I closed my eyes and said through tears:

"Thank you for saving Trey's life again, Dr. Mimms. Just tell me what we have to do to make him feel safe and to make you feel comfortable that he's safe." Dr. Mimms looked at me with gratitude and appreciation and also, as an equal participant in the madness of the NICU – sharing in decisions that shouldn't have to be made; procedures that shouldn't have to be done; words that should never be spoken; babies that shouldn't have been born and babies that shouldn't have died. We were on the same side of the disjointed world of the NICU and I realized that…

Dr. Mimms was a father, a husband, a brother, a son, an uncle, a colleague, a friend, a professor, a boss…oh, and by the way, he was also a doctor.

Steps to Living with Your Baby's Healthcare Providers

1. **Challenge the doctor's recommendations constantly** until you are satisfied that what they are recommending is the best choice for your baby (see "A" for Advocate).

2. **When you feel your emotions getting the best of you during a conversation with a doctor,** just breathe and remember, you and your doctor have the same goal — to get your baby healthy enough to go home.

3. **In your head, you have a vision of what is "normal."** This should never supersede the reality of your situation.

4. **Most hospitals have several neonatologists on staff, all with different styles and specialties.** Find the one that you can relate to the best, connect with on a deeper level, and speak to truthfully and as a friend. Find a nurse that you can develop a similar relationship with. These two providers will be your source of strength, information, and your reality check. Each and every day, you should…

5. **Bless them and love them.**

E: Educate Yourself

*You will be a stronger parent and advocate for your child if you
ask the right questions of your baby's healthcare provider.
Don't seek to be an expert, for that is the doctor's responsibility.
Seek to be informed. That is yours.*

From the minute you step foot in the NICU, you are inundated with information – things that you never thought you'd know or need to know. You will be asked to use this information to make decisions about the care of your child. Remember that the most important use of this information is in understanding how the topic impacts your baby, in the short-term and the long-term. You are not to be an expert, only informed enough to ask the right questions so that you can get the information you need to be a strong advocate for your baby. Although your questions will vary based on the situation, here are a few questions you could ask in any situation:

- What would happen if my baby did not get this procedure?

- Does it have to be done right now or can we wait until the baby is bigger/stronger/able to___? (Fill in a benchmark that would make this easier on the baby — from a procedural standpoint, from a recovery standpoint, or in terms of a delay that would increase the likelihood of a successful outcome.)

- What are the potential risks associated with this procedure? The doctors and nurses will likely review these with you if you are required to sign a consent form.

- Is this doctor/surgeon/specialist the best one to do this procedure?

- Where can I get more information on your recommendation?

The following are my all-time favorite questions. Ask them with confidence and be open to the answers.

- "If this were your child, doctor, would you do this procedure?"

- " Would you do this procedure now?"

- "Who would you have perform the procedure?"

- "Where would you have the procedure done?"

- "If you were me, what questions would you be asking right now?"

TAMI TIME

Regardless of what the doctors and nurses tell you, there are few decisions that need to be made instantaneously. If you don't have enough information to ask good questions and you need some time to educate yourself, tell the doctor that you would like to reconvene the next day so that you can ask more questions. During my entire journey, I never had to make any decisions on the spot. Even, for example, when Dr. Mimms told me that it was critically important that Trey have a tracheostomy immediately, I told him I needed some time. He gave me the afternoon — enough time to make two calls — one to a family friend who is a pediatric surgeon so I could get her perspective on the procedure...for Trey. The other was to a mother of a child who had a trach in place — so I could get her perspective on the emotional aspects of the procedure...for me.

Beware of the Internet! It is chock full of information — that is totally irrelevant to your situation. Reading the wrong Web site or accepting the wrong person as an authority will lead you to places that you should not be, to conclusions that should not be drawn, and into experiences that are not yours.

There are many Web sites out there dedicated to providing information on premature babies. Unfortunately, these sites are not reviewed or regulated. There are sites developed by parents; some launched by large companies that are trying to sell their products; others created by nurses, doctors, and hospitals; and even Web sites that are developed by the across-the-street neighbor of a guy, who had a friend, whose second cousin met a person in the grocery store once, who had a sister who had a premature baby. Do you get my drift?

Do not seek to get a degree in the NICU. Aim to get your degree in advocacy.

 PREEMIE PARENT **PRESENT:** A list of useful Web sites and books can be found in the "Resources" section at the back of this book and at www.preemieparents.com.

Steps to Educate Yourself

1. I found that the best book on the medical aspects of the NICU is *Preemies: The Essential Guide for Parents of Premature Babies,* by Dana Wechsler Linden, Emma Trenti Paroli, and Mia Wechsler Doron, M.D. This book demystifies most medical situations and prepares you appropriately for what could happen. Do not read ahead! This is meant as a reference book. Read only the chapters that have information on a subject that you are currently dealing with or one that the doctors have indicated your baby is likely to face. There are numerous chapters that will not apply to you. Don't read them. You'll make yourself crazy with "what ifs." You'll no longer be in the present but live in fear of the future. Believe me. I know. I did that and it was the single biggest mistake I made.

2. When faced with a medical situation that you want more information about, do not get your initial information from Web sites developed by parents. They had their experience and you are having yours. If you feel compelled to "chat" with other parents, ask the medical staff or social worker for names and contact information for a family who has had a situation similar to your own. Call those parents. You will be closer to comparing apples to apples.

3. Use Web sites that are not developed by parents for medical information. Refer to the "Resources" section at the back of the book for Web sites developed by healthcare professionals.

F: Family —
Best Intentions But...

*Before you ended up in the NICU, your family was
your biggest support unit, your biggest nightmare, or some
combination of both. Whatever they were before, they will
be the same now. This is not the time to try and create
relationships that don't already exist.*

T he NICU experience is exhausting on all levels. It will take all
of your physical strength and emotional energy to make it
through this, no matter how long your baby stays in the NICU.
Although the experience brings some families closer together, in general,
now is not the time to work out family disputes or build bridges that did
not previously exist. I've talked to dozens of families and the majority
find that their relationships with family and friends remain the same or
become worse.

Why? Absolutely no one can appreciate the depth, profound significance,
and constant emotional roller coaster of the NICU experience, regardless
of how understanding someone might be. The details that you provide
to your family and friends at the end of each day will never be enough

to fully portray what actually happens in the worst of the NICU situations. They will also try and fix it, to make it better for you. They will do what families are supposed to do. They will also do what they have historically done.

For those who are reading this section and are confused, congratulations! You clearly have strong, supportive family relationships. Keep them. Cherish them and nurture them. For those who are reading this and are having family challenges, read on.

In an effort to be completely transparent, this section was by far the most difficult in all of *Preemie Parents* to write because I didn't want to reopen old wounds or hurt those people who are "closest" to me. Writing this section was more difficult than retelling my story or remembering the darkest times in the NICU because in order to help you, the reader, the most, I had to recall vividly the raw pain of abandonment that I felt from my own family as I walked my journey of prematurity with my twins. I had to feel it and then remember the tools I used to release it. I will preface this part of my story by saying that this isn't about blaming anyone or standing in judgment of behavior and actions that happened nearly five years ago. It's about sharing my story, in the hopes of helping you write yours.

While on hospitalized bed rest for five weeks, I had seven visitors — only three of them were family and none of those three were my immediate family. During the twins' stay in the NICU (and for Trey beyond the NICU), there were even fewer visitors. Some were very unexpected and unwelcome like the priest who came to give last rites…without my permission and at the request of the twins' paternal grandparents. Have you any idea the guilt I have for kicking a priest out of the NICU? None! My father and uncle came to see me after the twins were born to tell me in person that my grandmother had passed away. I asked if they could go and see the twins (since I wasn't allowed to) and they reluctantly agreed. Neither ever came back to the hospital after that.

It was, in fact, the passing of my grandmother that allowed me the greatest insight into my family and helped me to release all of the negativity that I felt towards them. My grandmother passed two days after the twins were born. Months later, my parents organized a reunion of sorts so that everyone could spend some time at my grandmother's Hartford, Connecticut mansion before they sold it. My twins were three months old at that point, both still hospitalized and Trey was in the poorest condition he'd been in since birth. The date was chosen without consulting with me and it happened to be the day before Trey was to have his tracheostomy surgery. When I told my parents that I couldn't make it, they reminded me that my brother was flying in from California, my other brother was coming from Baltimore and, generally, *everyone* was making an effort to get there, so why couldn't I? They put so much pressure on me to come that I left the hospital at 9:00p.m., went home to get my older kids, and then drove the two hours to Hartford, arriving just in time for the stroke of midnight. I also knew full-well that I had to leave by 3:00 a.m. to make it back to the hospital in time for Trey's 6:00 a.m. pre-op call. Everyone at the reunion knew this, too, and no one cared. I was simmering the entire drive and when I arrived, everyone was drinking, dancing, and having a great time. I immediately knew that going there was a mistake.

At one point, my sister-in-law, Simone, found me alone in the kitchen and she asked about the twins. I told her about Trey's surgery the next morning and that I was feeling overwhelming anger and disgust at the family and that I was nauseous over the entire thing. We were both then summoned into the dining room, where nearly twenty of my family members sat around telling stories. Not one person asked about the twins. No one asked how I was holding up or how my kids were doing for that matter. Not one.

Simone finally said, "Why didn't we have this gathering in Morristown at the hospital? We all know that Trey is having surgery tomorrow." Everyone got very quiet and looked at me. I stared back with fire in my eyes and wishing that I had one of those great families that showed up at the NICU with care and concern. Actually, at that point, I wished for a family that just showed up.

I finally said to my parents, "And while we're on the subject, why haven't you been to the hospital to see Bria and Trey?"

They looked at each other and my Dad, an extremely educated man, said, "We don't want to get close to them in case they die. You know, so we can support you."

I said simply, "If they died, you'd be the last people I'd call." I then stood, packed my kids, and left. I didn't talk to any of my relatives for nearly two years — only mandatory communication and only by email. I even stopped attending family holidays and started my own at home. It was on my drive home from Connecticut that night that I became clear about my emotional boundaries, my lack of tolerance for nonsense, and I remembered my promise to be a strong mother for my kids. I recognized in that moment that I had been very weak in allowing other people to control my emotions for so long.

I pray that you do not have a situation like mine but if you do (in fact, even if you don't), here's a few life lessons I learned that night that helped me release all of the anger, hurt, disgust, disappointment, and general feelings of apathy about my family.

1. Everyone has free will. It was not my place to judge their decisions, actions, words, or feelings about my situation. After all, it was *my* situation.

2. Based on my experience that night, it was actually in my children's greatest good for them to be absent during our journey.

3. Even though they weren't acting as I would have liked, my family was simply doing the best they could at the time.

4. I learned a profoundly important parenting lesson that I couldn't have learned any other way and I carry with me still today — unconditional support for my kids is more important than any emotion I'm feeling.

5. Gorgeous flowers in any garden must be acknowledged, regardless of

their number and what surrounds them. Thank you Shandrea, Simone, Camari, Daryl, Amber, Aunt Michelle, and Uncle John.

At the writing of *Preemie Parents*, I've welcomed my family back into my life on my terms. I will never revisit the past with them because it doesn't serve anyone. While I still maintain my emotional boundaries, I've received my learning and I'm resolved.

That said, most family and friends want to help or at least feel helpful. I found that my closest friends and family really wanted to help me somehow; to contribute to the well-being of the twins for whatever reason. It is not for us to manage the emotions of others around this desire to help. Find ways for them to contribute to your journey and in doing so, move them along their own.

You must save your energy for bigger purposes.

Steps to Dealing with Family/Friends

1. Whatever experiences you've had with your family and friends in the past are just that — in the past. Now is not the time to deal with old issues.

2. Make a list of things that can be done without your oversight so that when people say, "What can I do to help?" you have an answer that helps them feel useful and helps you, as well. My mom happened to call me on the day the nurses said that I could put clothes on Bria. Having purchased nothing due to their unexpected arrival, I immediately tried to figure out when I would have time to find a place with preemie clothes and then time to actually shop. I told her I had a job for her. A full preemie wardrobe arrived in the mail two days later. Thanks, Mom! Need some other ideas?

- Grocery shopping

- Home-cooked meals for your family

- Purchasing gifts on your behalf for birthdays, anniversaries, graduations, etc.

- Babysitting for older siblings

- Buying you books, magazines, or newspapers for your NICU visits

- Buying you disposable cameras to keep under your baby's isolettes

- Writing thank-you notes for baby gifts (sound a bit too hands-off?). All right! How about just addressing the envelopes?

- Doing laundry

- Watering and weeding your garden and houseplants

- Acting as the go-between for you and your family and friends via email or a blog

3. Keep in touch in whatever way possible — I did email blasts every month. I know parents that set up Web sites to communicate with their families. Blogging has become very popular. Whatever you decide, stick to the Principles of P.E.A.C.E, provide just the facts and the good news.

4. Choose just a few people who you are close to and to whom you can turn without hesitation — people or a person who can handle the emotional rainfall of your experience. Divide your stories among them so they too have a chance to recover, get balanced, and are ready to support you for another day.

G: Gratitude: Spread It Thick and Often

The NICU reality can be transformed from one of fear and foreboding to one that promises tremendous happiness by using the power of gratitude. When you are tuned in to gratitude, you are actually attracting uplifting and healing frequencies into your life! These frequencies emanate from you and surround your baby in a healing light. So live with an attitude of gratitude.

You need as much inner strength as possible during your stay in the NICU. One source of this strength is through an intangible source called gratitude. Gratitude enables us to focus on the gifts we have; the gifts that we have accumulated and earned through our efforts; and the gifts that evoke happiness simply by thinking of them and having them in our minds. As the Law of Attraction states, "What you are thinking about most is also what you are attracting into your life at that very moment."

Thank everyone for everything — doctors, nurses, social workers, other parents…everyone. Whether a doctor has just delivered bad news or a nurse has put in an IV, your first words should always be "thank you" (refer to "D" for more on this). It may be difficult for you to feel grateful for this experience. That's why it is important to practice gratitude for every little thing, for, as you begin down this path, the larger experience will come into better focus. Ultimately, you will be thankful for the gifts the NICU has presented to you. Whether you choose to accept them is up to you.

"Gratitude unlocks the fullness of life. It turns what we have into enough, and more. It turns denial into acceptance, chaos into order, confusion into clarity.... It turns problems into gifts, failures into success, the unexpected into perfect timing, and mistakes into important events. Gratitude makes sense of our past, brings peace for today and creates a vision for tomorrow."

– Melody Beattie

TAMI TIME

I remember sitting at my son's side while he was in the warmer waiting to have his PDA surgery. There were IVs everywhere. He was already intubated. His charts were ready. He was packed to go. I said to Gail, my son's primary nurse, "If I could just hold him for a minute, this will go much better for both of us." Without hesitation, she began removing tubes, got a chair and a screen, and turned the lights out. She handed me my son and before I could say "thank you," the tears started streaming down my face. And then they came to take him. My heart was full of gratitude for her. When I finally got a chance to thank her, she said simply, "You already thanked me. You said it with your eyes."

Steps to Living in Gratitude in the NICU

1. **Celebrate and be thankful for every success** — no matter how big or small.

2. **Find reasons to be thankful for the entire NICU experience,** for each day you live it — you are stronger for it.

3. **In your journal,** list 5 things that you are grateful for every day.

H: Humor

In the middle of what might be the most difficult trial you have ever faced, maintaining your sense of humor probably seems ridiculous. Bill Cosby once said, "Through humor, you can soften some of the worst blows that life delivers. And once you find laughter, no matter how painful your situation might be, you can survive it." He is so very right.

I lived through my twins' surgeries, procedures, infections, days where it was touch and go and with my son, Trey, months of living the unknown. Through it all, I maintained my sense of humor. I am not a psychologist but I am certain that laughter opens your heart to receive gifts, messages, and blessings. Laughter causes connections, even if only for a moment, between people who might otherwise miss the opportunity to relate and grow together. Yes, I believe that laughter is the best medicine.

I remember sitting in the NICU, holding Trey late one November afternoon. He was asleep and I was reading. I could feel the herd of doctors and residents coming before I actually saw them. Here they came, a group of no less than fourteen providers coming to deliver news that was surely bad based on their faces. The attending physician, who had only been with the practice for a few weeks, was about to get right into it.

I said, "Just wait a second, doctor, so I can put Trey down." I had a rule that any conversation about Trey's health was not to be had over, at, or near his crib. I put him down and stepped away from his crib, forcing the entire posse to follow me. "OK. Now what is it that requires the presence of every single resident in the hospital to listen?" I scanned the group quickly and then turned back to the new attending, "I don't know you well. Look at this crowd around you! Are you some sort of rock star in Argentina?" There were smiles from the group.

"Ms. Gaines, we did an echocardiograph of Trey's heart today and the news is not good. Because his pulmonary hypertension is so severe, it is causing his heart to work harder. His right ventricle is severely enlarged and is putting additional pressure on the left ventricle. Trey is in the early stages of heart failure and we must treat him like he's on the verge of having a stroke." He paused to let this sink in. "Do you have any questions?"

"What's the good news?" I asked tentatively.

"Did I say there was good news?" he replied.

"Doctor, there is always good news," I answered. "Make something up."

He hesitated, "Well, we caught it early enough to try and manage it but there are no guarantees."

I went directly into my "advocate" mode. "So how do we treat him?"

"We need to stop some of his medicine and start him on others. I'll need your permission to use Sildenifil. It's been used successfully in trials with cardiac adult patients and in most cases, has been shown to reduce the pressure in the heart, reducing the likelihood of stroke or heart attack."

"What is Sildenifil?" I asked.

"Well, you might know it by its street name, Viagra. Dealing with sexual dysfunction is just one of its many uses. I'd like to start him on it right away."

"And how long does he need to stay on it?" I asked.

"For a long time. Until his lungs are healed," he responded quietly.

I thought about this for a minute and then looked at him. "First the ventilator, then the PDA repair, and then the tracheostomy, and then the G-Tube and now a lifetime of Viagra? This is just exactly what Trey needs on top of everything else — a permanent erection."

Everyone laughed, including me and suddenly, this group of strangers that came to tell me this terrible news about Trey's heart, realized that we were all in this together. We also knew that he would be just fine.

Steps to Maintaining Your Sense of Humor

1. Take the situation seriously but not yourself.

2. Don't force it. Sometimes just finding humor in the absurdity of it all is enough.

3. Research shows that the capacity for laughter came before the ability to speak. When in doubt, lead with your heart. Who cares if the doctors think you're crazy?

I: Take Care of "I"

You can take care of no one else unless you take care of yourself. It's just that simple.

During your NICU stay, you may feel that your priority is taking care of everyone else — your baby, your partner or spouse, your other children (if you have other kids), or even your pet. It is easy to forget to take care of yourself and it is also dangerous.

With two kids at home, traveling to the hospital daily (thirty minutes each way), and going through a separation from my husband, I was under such an extreme amount of stress that just finding time and energy to brush my teeth in the morning was an accomplishment. I lost thirty-five pounds (my baby weight and then some), had no muscle tone, and was barely sleeping. There came a day when I couldn't even lift my head off the pillow when I woke in the morning. I called my cousin, Camari, for relief and she came and entertained the kids. I slept all day and all night and most of the next day.

When I finally awoke and made my way downstairs, Camari said in a no-nonsense manner, "This is not good and you know what I mean."

She was right and I took immediate action. I made a commitment to take care of myself so that I could take care of my family. I began to walk around the park, became more consistent in my supplement routine, and even took greater care with my appearance — getting haircuts regularly, getting my nails done, and even moving from sweatpants to "real" clothes. I figured that if I looked good, then I would feel good and it worked.

Every week, I made time for something I enjoyed doing — not running errands, grocery shopping, or paying bills — something that made me feel like I was more than a mom with twins in the NICU. Once, I went to the beach and meditated by the water. Every now and then, I treated myself to dinner out. I even saw a few movies in the middle of the day while the twins were napping in the NICU. I realized the hard way that I couldn't be good for anyone else if I wasn't good to myself.

TAMI TIME

During my NICU journey, my eating habits went from bad to worse. I barely ate and if I did it wasn't sitting down for a good meal. I decided to eat a little bit all day long — "grazing" through the ups and downs of day. I always carried yogurt, trail mix, water, and some fruit. Once a day, I'd force myself to sit down somewhere and have a "fork and knife" meal, not for taste but for sustenance.

Steps for Taking Care of "I"

I. Eat well and often. Even "grazing" throughout the day is better than skipping meals completely. Focus on fresh, organic foods so that your body can replenish its energy quickly and efficiently. While fast food may be tempting, it's only empty calories that won't contribute anything to the health of your body.

2. Take nutritional supplements — B vitamins for energy, mental acuity, and endurance; Calcium for strength; Vitamin C to maintain your immune defenses; antioxidants to keep your blood and body clean and pure. My supplement regime was extensive.

3. Exercise daily, even if that means taking the stairs instead of the elevator while in the hospital. Park in the farthest part of the parking lot so you can walk a bit before and after your visit.

 PREEMIE PARENTS **PRESENT:** My NICU exercise and nutritional supplement regime are in the "Resources" section of this book and online at www.preemieparents.com.

4. Meditate, pray, or find some way to quiet your mind for at least ten minutes at the beginning and end of each day. This takes practice and you will find your own style.

5. As you pack the bag you bring to the NICU each day, be sure to include a few items that are just about you. I always packed my Walkman, favorite CDs, liquid Sage (for quick attitude changes), and an inspirational book (like this one!).

6. If you're feeling overwhelmed, talk to the NICU social worker or psychologist. There's nothing wrong with seeking professional help.

J: The Journey

"Our greatest and deepest wisdom is not given to us. It is discovered as we experience the journey that is ours and ours alone to take." —Tami C. Gaines

Most parents of premature babies would agree that having their baby admitted to the NICU was something that they hadn't anticipated or even considered. It certainly was not on my radar at the beginning of my pregnancy and when it happened, I was quick to accept it. It was through my spiritual guides, readings, and experiences that I'd long ago adopted a philosophy that all of life is a journey. The NICU is just another part of that path. *The best day of your premature baby's life might be the day you recognize and embrace the NICU journey as a tremendous opportunity for personal growth and enlightenment.*

I remember the very first time that I floated this concept to several women in the breastfeeding room. I was behind a curtain pumping, there was a woman behind the other curtain, and one waiting for us to finish. Anonymously, I offered the concept of the NICU being a great opportunity for personal growth. They were very, very quiet and one asked incredulously, "Are you proposing that our babies being born early or being sick is actually a good thing?" "No" I responded quickly. "Then what are you saying?" "I guess I'm saying that there's something about this craziness that feels divinely intentioned." That was a conversation-stopper for them but here, I'd like to use it as a jumping-off point for your growth.

Every major experience I've gone through has arrived, evolved, and resolved in seasons. As day follows night, so does each season change predictably.

My experience of prematurity began in the winter. It was February 14th, Valentine's Day, when I first went into pre-term labor. The dark days and cold nights of winter seemed to last forever. The coldness of fear settled over me and seeped into me, with each passing day on bed rest. When March came, I could see spring coming through my small hospital window. The twins were born on March 21st, the spring equinox — a time when dormant growth comes alive and the buds of new growth emerge. Both twins came home in the summer (although a year apart), a season of warmth, joy and carefree living. And as a family, we settled into fall — a celebration of the harvest, bountiful blessing, and abundance.

You are in a season right now. As you move from one season to the next, your opportunities for growth increase and your accomplishments become larger. I believe this journey requires courage, faith, and preparation.

ON COURAGE...
Courage is taking action with confidence, in spite of your doubt and fear. The idea of "strength" is explored in the "S" section of this book. But courage and strength are not the same thing. Courage requires taming your fear. Fear is simply the anticipation of pain. If you live in a place of fear during your NICU journey, your ability to support yourself and your family through this ordeal will be nearly impossible. Don't let your fear take you off course. Your fear is just a story that your mind has created to protect you from your reality.

My mind is very tricky. It wove a very elaborate story to protect me from my reality: that I was a woman who was going through a divorce, with two children at home and two babies in the hospital. Fundamentally, that was my reality. The story my mind created went something like this: "You are a woman who wasn't good enough for your husband, so he left you. You aren't a good mom to the two kids you have now and that's why he didn't want to have any more kids. Your life will be devastated if you get divorced so you should do all you can, even if it doesn't serve you, to stay married. Your kids at home will be permanently scarred emotionally from this experience so protect them from all things and coddle them as much as possible. Finally, there's a good chance that your two babies in the hospital will die any day so you should just sit around and wait for that to happen. And by the way, if they do live, you'll be alone forever because who would want you with four kids? How will you ever support yourself?" And on and on and on…

I lived from that story for a time. I soaked in it like a bath and I was sad and scared but comfortable…just as my mind had intended me to be. I lost my appetite, lost weight, couldn't sleep, and nearly lost my mind thinking of the "what ifs" of my life. There came a time when I was sitting in the kitchen staring into the nothingness in front of me, completely caught up in my own emotional decay. I hadn't heard my older daughter come in, but I could feel her staring at me. I turned and met her gaze, the tears beginning to form in her eyes. I realized that she was waiting for me to fall apart — just as the rest of her life seemingly had. In the silence between us, she pleaded with me to hold it together because that was the only way that she could find the courage to believe in the simplest…possibility.

It was in that one moment, a split-second of clarity, that I made a decision to rewrite my fear-based story and replace it with a more empowering one — for my sake and for the sake of my children. The writing of the story was relatively easy. I took my journal to the park and wrote of the woman that I could be — the rock that we all needed to keep going. I wrote of my past accomplishments, my strong points, moments when I'd won against all odds. I recounted the times in my life when I felt the most powerful. I wrote, humorously, about the ridiculous time I'd wasted living in fear of the unknown — things that may or may not happen. I wrote of the woman that I would become and made a commitment to spend every minute becoming that person.

Of course, becoming that person was much more difficult. Our minds are gardens and anything we plant there will grow, good or bad. Through reading self-help books, personal development exercises, meditation, journaling of my successes and stumblings, ongoing self-assessment, heightened self-awareness and awareness of the help of many spiritual, healers, I gave up my unsupportive story. I started telling myself tales of worthiness, self-love, extraordinary parenting, self-confidence, and emotional, spiritual, and financial independence. I transformed into the woman that I wrote about in my journal. I looked in the mirror several times a day — not out of vanity but as a reminder to myself to see who I was becoming. I had to fight against the world around me that wanted to change my mind — that wanted me to take the easy out and go back to the old story. But those characters didn't serve me anymore; the plot was stuck and the ending…well, that was still unknown.

My daughter began to show signs of her old self. My older son had fewer temper tantrums. That new story, the one that I chose to live from, is the story that allowed everything after it to happen. It's how I came to the NICU with a smile on my face daily and the courage to confront whatever lay beyond the entry door.

ON FAITH…

The second part of my formula is developing a journey that you walk in faith. Faith that everything is exactly as it is intended to be. Faith that you are strong enough right now to get through this. Faith that your baby's journey is connected to yours, but is ultimately separate. You must live, even if your baby doesn't. It is having faith that makes you act in spite of.

I had many tests of faith but perhaps the greatest was when Trey had his G-Tube (gastrostomy tube) placed. I said "goodbye" to him and watched him disappear into the operating room. I was on the phone with my sister-in-law (my long distance support), when a resident came running out, pale and shaken, and told me that Trey had flatlined on the table, after they'd administered the anesthesia. And just as quickly he ran back in the room. Shandrea heard the exchange on the other end of the phone and fell silent as we both waited for someone to come out and tell me that all was well. They didn't for quite awhile. I heard myself telling Shandrea, "They are great doctors. Trey is very strong. He's come through so much. He knows how much he is loved and I believe that he will choose to stay here." I heard myself telling her these things and I realized that it wasn't my brain speaking. It was my heart. It was the deep-seated faith I'd developed in Trey's resiliency, in his healthcare providers, and in our journey that inspired those words. The doctors walked slowly out of the room, followed by the nurses wheeling Trey back to the NICU. Dr. Feldman came to me and said simply, "I don't know what happened. I just don't know. One minute he was fine and the next, we'd lost him." With great compassion and appreciation for her and her team, I asked, "He's OK now, right?" She nodded. "Well," I said, "that's all that matters." As I was hanging up with Shandrea, she said, "You are an amazing woman." I told her that we are all amazing. You are, too.

ON PREPARATION...

The final piece of my puzzle was preparation. You can't be prepared for everything but you can be prepared for anything — mentally, physically, and spiritually. We've previously discussed exercise and nutrition (see page 61) — physical preparation. The discussion above on fear and faith are both forms of mental and spiritual preparation. There is one very simple philosophy that you must adopt as quickly as possible in order to be fully prepared, at all times, for absolutely anything that comes your way. It's simple but it's not easy. It requires courage and faith to embrace it and live from its enlightened place.

The situation you are facing is not the problem.
It's your thoughts and the story you tell yourself
about the situation that is the problem.
It's your reaction to your thoughts and your story that is the problem.
Don't believe your own thoughts. Separate yourself from them.
And then you will find your true power in any situation.

Do you believe me? You ought to. I am not your thoughts. They are the ones you must not believe! Please sit with that concept for awhile. Meditate on it. Write it on a piece of paper and carry it with you everywhere. Let it be a constant reminder of your opportunity for growth.

This is your journey and it was predestined by the Universe. There is no sense fighting against it. The quicker you accept your place in the NICU, the faster your world will begin to stabilize. No matter how tumultuous your life might seem right now, it will move back into balance. After all, being in balance is the natural order of things.

Steps to Mastering Your Journey

1. **Recall the Principles of P.E.A.C.E.** (refer to pages 12-13).

2. **Trust yourself.**

3. **Embrace your challenges,** for it is through them that you will see your true possibility.

4. **Stand strong,** because you are strong.

5. **Just take one step at a time.**

6. **Ask yourself,** "Who will be stronger? Me or my problems?"

7. **Ask yourself,** "How did I grow through that experience?"

8. **See things as they are** — not worse than they are and not better than they are.

9. **Have a vision of yourself** beyond your current circumstances.

10. **In the winter season, go skiing.**

K: Kangaroo Care
Is Critical Care

*In Bogota, Columbia, two doctors discovered that in the absence
of life-saving technology, simply having babies held skin-to-skin,
in an upright position with the baby's head positioned to hear the
parent's heartbeat, caused the mortality rate among preemies
to decrease from 70 percent to 30 percent. They called this
"kangarooing." The benefits are undeniable but in the
NICU it can sometimes be daunting.*

The benefits of "kangaroo care" are enormous. If your baby is in a NICU that doesn't encourage it or, in fact, discourages it, take matters into your own hands and ADVOCATE. Research shows that babies who receive kangaroo care on a regular basis receive numerous benefits, including:

- Better sleep
- Less colic
- Reduced episodes of apnea

- Higher oxygen saturations

- More regular respiration and heartbeat

- Increased ability to maintain body temperature

- Higher weight gain

- Shorter hospital stays

- Improved lactation for Moms

You know all of this and you want to, but how? Your baby looks so small and so fragile. In the littlest ones, their skin is so thin that it is sensitive to the touch. The number of tubes and wires seem impossible to manage. This is where your ability to have Intention (see "I") becomes incredibly important. Have the nurse help you get comfortable in a rocking chair with your baby. Take yourself and your baby to another place mentally — in a rocking chair in the nursery in your home; to a seat on a veranda; to a swing on a porch — whatever scene makes you feel relaxed and energized. Your baby will pick up every vibration you send off while kangarooing so give him good ones! Relax and enjoy it.

TAMI TIME

The best day I ever had in the NICU was when I was unexpectedly allowed to kangaroo both babies at the same time. It took about 15 minutes and two nurses to get them situated, moving wires and tubes so that they could get as flat on my chest as possible. I put my walkman on and turned up the reggae music. On that particular day, we were all going to Jamaica. I had a little smile on my face as I held Bria and Trey close and turned my face up to the imaginary sun. All that was missing was our bathing suits and sunscreen. The three of us slept like that for what seemed like hours but, in fact, it was only about ten minutes. I hold on to that memory because one day we will all sit on the white sand beaches of Negril — equipment-free, and I'll tell them "you know, you were here before!"

Steps to Kangaroo Care with Your Baby

1. **Ask your nurse to remove all non-essential wires and tubes so that you can have a bit more freedom to snuggle** — even if they only take them off for 5-10 minutes.

2. **Always wear shirts or blouses with buttons down the front when you visit** so you can be skin-to-skin easier.

3. **Don't wear fragrances or perfumes when you visit.**

4. **Ask the nurses to turn down or turn off the lights if possible.**

5. **Look for a rocking chair** or the most comfortable chair you can find.

6. **Ask for a screen for privacy.**

7. **Once your baby is positioned,** slouch down so you can simulate being reclined. Breathe deeply for several minutes to relax yourself and to slow your heartbeat.

8. **Just be.** Find your happy place and enjoy.

L: Listen to Your Instincts

You don't have to be a doctor or nurse to know what's best for your baby. A feeling inside of you; a small voice in the back of your head; even an indescribable nagging will always lead you to the right answer. Don't ignore it. Explore it and go with it.

As a parent, you know what's best for your child in all circumstances, whether you believe it and acknowledge it or not. In the NICU, it is so easy to get into the rational, analytical part of your brain when there are decisions to be made. But more often than not, your snap decision will be the right one.

Each morning, upon arriving in the NICU, I'd scrutinize both babies, looking for anything different than the day before. When Bria opened her eyes and looked at me, on one particular morning, I just knew something was wrong. There was no spark in her eyes and she just seemed different. Granted, she was only three weeks old — and barely two pounds. I didn't know her well but I knew her well enough to know that she wasn't feeling good. I asked the nurses about it and they said her vitals were all fine, she was eating well, pooping well, and that all was normal. I insisted that it wasn't but they kept referring to their charts and telling me that everything was normal. About three hours later, Bria spiked a very high fever and began desatting. She required more oxygen and couldn't keep her food down. As it turned out, Bria got a terrible infection that took weeks to treat.

In the absence of certainty, always trust your instincts. You are born with instincts to help you survive. And remember that it is all right if you can't put it into words. Just trust your instincts.

TAMI TIME

I struggled with the decision on whether or not to bring my two older kids to see their NICU siblings.

The children were so excited when I finally told them I was pregnant with twins — a little brother and sister — one for each of them! And then I was placed on hospitalized bed rest to stay pregnant and I told them, "It's not the twins' fault." And then their father left and I told them, "It's not anyone's fault." And then the twins were born early and I told them, "It's not anyone's fault." And when I saw the twins laying in the isolettes, so small that instead of diapers, the hospital used cotton balls, I wanted to shield my two older kids from this at all costs. It was scary and it was not anybody's fault. But with the uncertainty of survival in those early days, they had to see them. I didn't want my two older kids to be subjected to any more sadness. Back and forth I went and I finally allowed my instincts to guide me. "Bring them," my soul said. And so I did, reluctantly. When my daughter looked in the isolette, she said, "They are so small and cute." My son said, "Hi. I'm your big brother." And I cried for their innocence and devotion and unconditional love. The very best days we ever had in the NICU were the days when Haili and Shane came to visit.

Steps to Listening to Your Instincts

1. **Practice thinking with your heart instead of your head.**

2. **Practice making snap decisions,** behave automatically and effortlessly.

3. **Instincts often help habits develop.** Create habits of natural action.

M: Money Is an Object

Some think money is private. Others think money is dirty.
Whatever your thoughts about money, in the case of the
NICU money is an object and the only value it has is
that which you place on it.

Depending on the length of your baby's stay, your NICU journey will cost from $10,000 to many hundreds of thousands of dollars. Having anxiety about the price tag is not a good use of your time or energy since there is absolutely nothing you can do about it. You can't speed up your baby's stay. You can't tell the doctor's to order fewer tests or prescribe less medicine. All you can do is know that the costs will be what they are. At the writing of this book, my twins' medical bills were more than a million dollars and climbing. I haven't lost a night of sleep over it because it is what it is. And everyone will get paid eventually, somehow.

What I have spent some time thinking about is that although money is an object, money has matter — and money matters need to be dealt with. I watched far too many parents have to leave their baby to go back to work, limit their visits to lunchtime and after work, or miss days completely. One of the worst days I had in the NICU was watching a father come for his visit after getting off of work, only to learn of the imminent death of his baby. I couldn't quite read the look on his face. It was a mix of helplessness and guilt, shadowed by the recognition that he missed critical time with his baby…perhaps that he should have skipped work that day? He was doing what he had to do to support his family by going to work, yet in doing so, he missed the opportunity to do what he was meant to do — and that was to be with his wife in the last hours of his baby's life. The pursuit of money should never be a reason to leave critically ill babies. It appears that we all need to be better prepared financially before something catastrophic happens. What follows is a crash course in money matters and what I hope will be the starting point for another positive journey for you.

MY MONEY STORY

I was raised in an upper-income family, where speaking of money was taboo. Because of this, I was financially illiterate. In fact, even after graduating from Columbia University's Graduate School of Business, I was no closer to learning how to create real wealth than before I went. After becoming pregnant with my oldest daughter, I quit Corporate America and started my own consulting firm. The firm grew to 25 full-time and part-time employees, with sales of over half-a-million dollars. After the events of September 11th, every one of my clients (all early-stage technology companies), lost their funding and I found myself with nearly $200,000 in receivables that I'd never collect and just over $100,000 in debt that I had no way to pay. As Charles Dickens said, "It was the best of times. It was the worst of times." I was emotionally, financially, and spiritually devastated. I'd never been in that kind of money trouble before and had other people relying on me to figure it all out. After three months, I pulled my head out of the sand and decided to deal with the inevitable. I laid off my employees, negotiated with debtors as much as I could, and re-evaluated how I was making my money.

TAMI TIME

I remember when it was time to take Bria home. At that point, we owed $30,000 after insurance! I only half-jokingly asked if I had to pay for her in full before they gave her to me! Thank goodness they can't repossess kids!

That was the end of the pity party and the beginning of my wealth journey. I became committed (almost obsessed) with becoming financially free — a point where my passive income exceeded my expenses. I realized that my consulting company was just a great job. My income was totally dependent on my next client and there was no cash-machine built into it. I met with my investors and millionaire mentors to learn how to change my thinking and my habits to act as wealthy people do. Those conversations led me to wealth-building seminars and books like *Think and Grow Rich, Rich Dad, Poor Dad,* and my all-time favorite, *The Secrets of the Millionaire Mind.* I became financially literate and armed with so much information, I was able to pay off my business' debt in three years and put financial structures in place that have set me on the path to financial freedom. Now I spend a lot of time teaching others how to do the same thing.

MONEY MATTERS

Being financially independent became critically important after my divorce. It's a terrible feeling being reliant on your ex for money. In our case, it just became another means for him to control me. I knew that in order to be financially independent, I would first have to become financially free. What is financial freedom? It's the ability to live the lifestyle you desire without having to work, or rely on anyone else for money. I know you're thinking, "That sounds great. How in the world do I do that?" There's a simple equation that I learned in *The Secrets of the Millionaire Mind.*

THE FINANCIAL FREEDOM FORMULA

Working Income + Savings + Investments + Passive Income + Simplification = Financial Freedom

I know…"what in the world does that mean?" I learned it in its most simple terms:

- Your **working income** is the money you make from your job *(or in my case my consulting business).* **+**

- The money you have **saved** *(even if it's under your mattress!)* **+**

- The money that's generated from **investment** interest from things like IRAs, mutual funds, real estate investments, etc., *(When I got divorced, all of our investments were liquidated — luckily before the market crashed!)* **+**

- **Passive income** or the money that just shows up in your mailbox from a business that you built at some point and it keeps paying you forever, with little effort on your part. *(I started a business in 2002 that I built for a few years and then the money just showed up. In fact, it showed up every Monday for two years while I was in the NICU. That allowed me to just be with the twins…and not worry about being with a boss.)* **+**

- **Simplifying** your financial life — putting systems and habits in place so your finances will run smoothly.

= FINANCIAL FREEDOM

When you have the Financial Freedom Formula in place, you will be financially free and you will also have time-freedom. Time-freedom and financial freedom are two things that would make anyone's NICU journey much more bearable. As I chatted with moms in the nursing room and heard their anxiety over money and leaving their babies to go back to work, I realized that we all need more financial education so we understand that money is an object and when things like the NICU appear on our monitor, money is one less thing to worry about.

 PREEMIE PARENT **PRESENT:** In the "Resources" section, I've provided a much more detailed explanation of financial freedom and I've included ideas to help you get started.

Steps to Money Matters in the NICU

1. Pull out your health insurance policy and find out what's covered, what's not, what the limitations are, the maximum out-of-pocket expenses, etc. Be informed, not surprised.

2. Meet with the insurance guru in the NICU (most have them) and discuss your baby's hospitalization, costs, and any expected issues with insurance coverage. This is also the time to discuss special needs and equipment that might be required upon discharge.

3. If you are employed by someone else, pull out your company's employee handbook to see what the policies are regarding disability, personal time off, vacation, etc. You'll need as much time as possible to be available for your baby — paid time off would be a bonus.

4. Use some of your NICU downtime to begin reading financial literacy books.

5. When you get through this — and you will get through this — commit to being financially free in preparation for whatever might come next. Something always comes next.

Dealing with Your Insurance Carrier

KNOW YOUR INSURANCE CARRIER

- Know the name of your insurance carrier and always carry your insurance card. It must have your member ID number, plan/group number, and customer service phone number printed on it.

- Know if the hospital and your doctors are "in-network" (better coverage) or "out-of-network" (higher out-of-pocket costs for you).

- Know if you need a referral form, authorization, or prescription for services.

- Know that even if the hospital and doctors are "in-network" for your insurance plan, it does not guarantee that the services will be covered.

- Check with your employer's Employee Benefits Representative (usually in the Human Resources department) to understand your benefits.

- If the NICU has an insurance manager, use this person for his/her expertise. These managers have a wealth of knowledge.

- Keep good records related to your baby's care.

KNOW HOW TO ADVOCATE FOR YOUR BABY

- Get everything in writing!

- Don't take the customer service representative's word for it. If you aren't getting the answer you want, ask to speak to a manager.

- Check your insurance company's Web site for information regarding your benefits.

- Keep a log of every conversation and contact with your insurance company — what was said; who said it; who initiated the contact; and when they said it.

- Always try and speak with the same person at your insurance company. If your case is complicated, request a case manager who will be your key contact. Be sure to give the name and number of this person to your baby's providers.

- If you think that payment was denied or processed incorrectly, use your insurance company's appeal process to have the decision investigated or possibly reversed.

A FEW QUESTIONS TO ASK YOUR INSURANCE CARRIER

- Do I need a referral for the baby's stay in the NICU?

- Is the hospital and/or doctors in-network?

- If an emergency procedure is required and pre-certification cannot be obtained, how is that handled?

- Do reimbursement checks come to me or directly to the provider?

- Can I have a case manager to help me with my insurance claims and questions?

- What can I do to simplify the process of working with you so it's one less thing to worry about?

N: Negativity Is Contagious

With a baby (or babies) in the NICU and all of the great mysteries that go along with it, you have every excuse to be negative, down, and generally pessimistic. There is only one overriding reason why you should not be negative. Negativity surrounds you and seeps into you like an infection that there's no prescription for. Just as you wash your hands before you enter the NICU to prevent the spread of germs to the babies, you must wash your attitude for the very same reason.

Everyone has gone negative at some point in their lives — it is common and an easy place to find yourself in. How do you know if you've gone negative on the NICU experience? Answer the following questions as honestly as possible:

1. Do you lack belief that your baby will get better?

2. Do you feel that life is unfair?

3. Do you feel like nothing will help or make a difference?

4. Do you feel lonely, defeated, or overwhelmed?

5. Do you put barriers between yourself and others — obstacles that are difficult to overcome?

If you answered "yes" to any of these questions, you might be feeling pessimistic or negative.

You wouldn't believe what made me go negative after that first month — the alarms and ringing bells on the equipment in the NICU! I felt like I was in a video arcade and my brain was the pinball. They ring all the time. Something is always alarming. Machines are always screaming for attention. It became too much and I resented going into the NICU. I had enough self-awareness to know that I had to reframe those darn machines so I could manage my daily visits. I realized that every time something rang, it was really yelling, "Get over here and save this kid's life!" I have learned to appreciate the machines for the role they play in the twins' lives… literally. I even named them: Vinnie the Vent(ilator); Pam the Pulsoximeter and Babbs the Ambu Bag that brought my kids back from the brink of death so many times. Honor the equipment and learn to love those ringing bells.

You may have something that triggers you or just have a general feeling of sadness. There is no shame in going negative; after all, you are experiencing what may be the most traumatic journey of your life. But the one big reason to work through it is for the sake of your

TAMI TIME

With two babies gravely ill for the first few months of their lives, I went negative often, wondering to myself if there was something more I could have done to prevent this. The worst times of day were first thing in the morning and right before bedtime — quiet time, when I had a chance to get inside of my own head and reflect on where I was in life. I made a conscious effort to leave all feelings of doubt, sorrow, and fear in the parking lot before I went to visit my twins. I often sprayed liquid Sage around my head to clear it of all negative emotions. Before I went into the NICU, I took several deep breaths, closed my eyes, and pictured the day that my four kids would be playing together in my backyard. I also made it clear that no bad news was to be delivered to me at or near the twins' crib and never in front of other families. I was adamant about this and would simply walk away if a nurse, resident, or doctor forgot my rule. My leaving would force them to follow me out of the NICU, where I was open and ready to receive information. It's not easy. Learn how to convert negativity into positive energy and your journey will be faster and smoother.

baby, the healthcare providers, and others that you come in contact with on a daily basis in the hospital.

Negativity enters a room before you do and stays long after you leave. Ask yourself if you are affecting people around you or if you are infecting them. I'm certainly not proposing that you be Homecoming King or Ms. Congeniality every day but I am suggesting that you do an attitude check before you enter the NICU.

Steps to Overcoming Negative Thoughts

1. **Identify the feelings** that you have before the negativity appears. Redirect them before the downward spiral begins.

2. **Memorize and embody the Principles of P.E.A.C.E.** There's comfort in just leaving everything in the hands of the Universe.

3. **Recognize that unresolved anger and misguided beliefs** often lead to negativity. Take time daily to identify and address issues at your core.

4. **Begin the hard work of building your self-esteem during this difficult period.** Remind yourself of what a tremendous mother or father you must be — your baby chose you! Tell yourself how strong you are every day that you get out of bed, get to the hospital, and support your baby — and then come home to do the same for your spouse, partner, and/or other children. You are superhuman, worthy of every blessing that life has to offer.

 PREEMIE PARENTS **PRESENT:** A list of heart and soul boosters can be found in the "Resources" section of this book and online at www.preemieparents.com.

5. **Seek professional help if you are having difficulty.** Most NICUs have social workers on staff that can work with you or refer you to a psychiatrist or therapist.

O: Observation and Self-Awareness

You might think it unusual, this conversation about "observation and self-awareness" in the context of the NICU experience. However, observation and self-awareness are ultimately about recognizing your behavior and emotions to determine whether they serve you in a particular situation. This is about mastering your emotions so that you can master this experience.

Mastering where we focus our attention and how we focus it is the key to our freedom during the NICU experience and it is the essence of self-awareness. What you focus on expands. Choosing what you focus on and how you react to it is to become self-aware. Like all else about the NICU, the art of observation and self-awareness is an incredible invitation to engage in self-reflection and discovery. Observation is the process of listening, studying, exploring, thinking, and questioning what we see and feel so that we have the opportunity to make choices instead of just reacting to our situation or environment.

Pay attention to how you feel physically, emotionally, the stories playing in your mind, and the thoughts you keep in your head. By observing yourself in this way, you are becoming self-aware. In the NICU setting, pay particular attention to stress as it happens and your reaction to it. By the way, others will notice your reaction to it also.

Early on in the NICU, I was told that the twins, assuming they lived through the first few weeks, would have a very long stay and that I should consider having a primary nurse for them. This was a new concept for me (and perhaps for you?). The simplest way to explain what a primary nurse is is to think of her/him as the best nanny your fairy godmother could possibly grant you! When they are working, they are with your baby. They come to know your baby as well as you do and, if you don't get to visit often for one reason or another, they may know your baby better than you do. This is not a case for jealousy…it's an opportunity for gratitude. Your baby's "primary" consults with the doctors, advocates for your baby, and is generally in total charge of your baby's entire growth and development. Overall, it's a very organic process. I started to gravitate toward certain nurses during the early weeks of our NICU journey. When it was time for me to choose a primary, it was like an interview process. They were checking me out and I was checking them out. Do we click? Do we like each other? Can we get along in stressful situations for what could be months? What are

TAMI TIME

I entered the NICU daily with a smile on my face, with hope in my heart, and a kind word for everyone who passed my way. One day, as I sat holding Trey, a perfect stranger walked by me and pushed my shoulders down. That simple act relaxed my entire body and made me aware that I was carrying my stress in my shoulders — not on my face or even in my head. It took a focused effort to recognize when my shoulders were raised and then an even greater effort to breathe through my stress, face my fears, and be clear about my concerns. My shoulders being up was a form of defense — I was constantly awaiting the next attack, be it bad news from the doctors, from a negative person in my life, or from within myself. Only when my shoulders were relaxed did I know that I'd accomplished self-awareness for the moment — this was a daily and sometimes hourly effort.

their values? Family situation? Work ethic? Experience? It all comes out through conversation and I happily had several to choose from for both babies. In an unusual turn of events, Bria and Trey had daytime primaries and nighttime primaries. And backup for those primaries. I felt so lucky to have them all and showed them as much gratitude as I could. They were the only reason that I got any sleep at night. I'm still in touch with many of them!

On the other hand, there were many families in the NICU that complained because they weren't assigned a primary. They moaned and groaned about the unfairness of it all. They asked to speak to supervisors and managers and demanded that someone work with them as primaries. I just wished that these parents caught themselves in a moment of…well… being themselves. They wouldn't have wanted to work with themselves either! They lacked self-awareness and, ultimately, they lacked primary caregivers, too.

Observing your emotions and shifting them leads to a certain quiet in your mind. It allows you to go calmly about your life, knowing that there is no attack coming. And if it does, you will continue to stay calm, listening, observing, and acting without overreacting. You will pause to connect with your inner self and relax in the knowledge that you and you alone are in control of your emotions.

Steps to Improving Observation and Self-Awareness

1. **Recognize how you are feeling and behaving.**

2. **Notice whether your actions are as you intended.** If not, correct them immediately.

3. **Ask yourself, "Where am I weak?" and "Where am I strong?"** Work on your weakest areas and proceed from your strengths.

4. **Begin to notice the patterns of your emotions** so that you can conquer them before they conquer you!

5. **Ask other people to help you** become more aware of patterns of behavior that don't serve you.

6. **Acknowledge your success and reward yourself** — this is hard work!

P: Personalization: Own the Experience

Sure, your baby is in an isolette in the neonatal intensive care unit of a hospital. But it's your baby, in his isolette in a hospital. Remember and honor that.

If you were home, anticipating the arrival of your baby, you'd be fixing up the spare room to make it look like the most fabulous nursery on the face of the earth! You might be picking out fabric for curtains, buying coordinating sheets for the crib, and filling the space with items that say to your baby, "You are ours. Welcome to the family!" Your nursery might have been completed before the baby was born. In either case, for the time being, the hospital is home. Do what you can to make it feel like…home.

Now, I'm not suggesting bringing in your glider and ottoman but there is so much else you can do to reflect your family's personality and celebration of your baby's birth. I added pictures of our home family to the isolettes — so the babies could see them. We were also given a bulletin board. On that board I hung pictures of our house, my intention (see "I"), hand-drawn pictures from Haili and Shane, my favorite poems, and funny cartoons. I added quotes and lots of colored streamers. You could tell from across the room where Bria and Trey were…it was the imaginary party room. And they were the center of attention. I know some folks in the NICU thought I was nuts, but who cared? If Bria and Trey were home, that's how they'd be living!

Home is where the heart is. And your heart is where your baby is.

Steps to Personalizing the Experience

1. **Bring photos of family, friends, pets** — anyone who your baby would be meeting if he was home.

2. **Bring receiving blankets that reflect your style or the nursery theme** — they can make up the baby's isolette or crib with them.

3. **If you have older children, encourage them to make pictures for the baby** — hang them up in the hospital.

4. **When your baby is able to wear clothes, bring your own.** Hospital kimonos are nice but hardly reflect the individual personality of your fabulous baby!

5. **If you are allowed, bring in a CD player with a CD** that you've compiled of all the music that your family loves.

TAMI TIME

My mother-in-law is the most amazing fiber artist you've ever met. She can crochet a kitchen table and knit the chairs! In anticipation of the arrival of the twins, she was hard at work on baby blankets, as she'd done with my two older kids. When the twins were born early and wouldn't be home, she was at a loss. Rather than break tradition, I asked her to make isolette covers. The nurses happily lent me one of the hospital's for measurements. The completed isolette covers were fabulous, all the rage in the NICU, if for no other reason than they looked like…home.

Q: Queen

Sorry, guys, this is for the moms in the audience…
Be what you are, a Queen.

How about a dose of girl power? Gentlemen, don't skip this chapter. It will give you some perspective on your wife, partner, sister, aunt or friend. She is a Queen, if only by definition. Just look at a few of my favorite definitions below.

Queen: (kwēn) noun

1. A woman sovereign or monarch.

You are the Queen of your castle, overseeing and managing all of the activities in your kingdom. You are due respect.

2. The most powerful chess piece, able to move in any direction over any number of empty squares in a straight line.

You are powerful, adaptable, and flexible in any number of situations. You are self-aware and positive — and you move right past empty squares to find the ones with your life lessons in them.

3. The fertile, fully developed female in a colony of social bees, ants, or termites.

Well, you're obviously fertile. Enough said.

4. **A woman who rules a country, who inherits her position by right of birth.**

In my story, there was no one to treat me like a queen. My husband was long gone. I didn't have anyone to say, "You are a queen today." But I didn't need one. Because I was/am one. Both of my grandmothers had trained me well in the fine art of royal leisure. They were the only two women I knew who could read the paper in their bathrobes, hair in rollers, and look like ladies of the court! I made a point of periodically and regally exiting the NICU to catch a movie, eat a meal out, or just read in my car. I was alone but no one was more worthy of these regal outings!

You are a Queen. You were born into this role and no one can take your place as you move royally through your journey.

THERE'S ONLY ONE STEP TO HONOR THE QUEEN
Be who you are. Acknowledge it daily even when others do not.

R: Release: Letting It All Go

"All healing is a release from the past." — Tami C. Gaines

After I told my then-husband that I was pregnant with twins, he let me know in no uncertain terms that he was leaving me and he did. My twins were delivered by emergency C-section on March 21st, because of a lethal blood infection that I'd acquired while on hospitalized bed rest. They were only 1 pound, 12 ounces and 1 pound, 13 ounces and just twenty-five weeks' gestation. A day later, my paternal grandmother passed away. She was my role model, having lived the life I imagined every day. With a 105° temperature for several days, violent tremors, recovering from the C-section, and no appetite, I had visits hourly from the infectious disease team because no one knew what was wrong with me or if I would even recover. It was without a doubt among the most difficult span of days that I'd ever experienced in my life. In and out of a fitful, drug-induced sleep, my fears came and went with consciousness. I had a sense that I had to let it all go, so that it didn't take me into a black hole, from which there'd be no escape. I had a simple conversation with God: "God, I'm tired and I'm tired of worrying about all of this. I surrender it to you. You figure it out and drop it back in my lap when it's resolved." There was something about that short talk we had, that made it seem better.

Letting go of your fears can help you face the unknown without faltering. Instead of preparing for some mysterious eventuality, the act of releasing allows us to just be. The frightening scenarios we create in our minds prevent us from living presently because the world seems fraught with peril. When you accept that the future is unknown, you are free to anticipate positive outcomes because they have just as good a chance of happening as do negative ones.

Let it all go. Give your fears to the angels. And they will return them to you unrecognizable, disguised as hope. Soften your heart with respect to your baby's stay in the NICU. Choose to live life with a sense of excitement and possibility about all the uncertainty in your life.

TAMI TIME

I love Stevie Wonder. Every important memory I have has a Stevie Wonder song playing in the background. One of his songs found its way into my CD player more than any other during my NICU journey — "Have A Talk With God." The words encourage the listener to give their concerns over to God, especially when they seem too enormous to manage. Somehow, that song always made me feel that even when I was alone, I wasn't. I also immersed myself in reading positive books, like *Conversations with God* and *The Prophet.* Finally, poetry or thought-provoking essays also helped me release. On page 95 of this book is a poem by a good friend of mine.

Steps to Releasing

1. **If you are afraid, just pray** to whoever or whatever carries significance for you.

2. **Be detached from the outcome.** Detachment is a powerful concept.

3. **Recognize those things that are out of your control —** which is just about everything in the NICU — and just flow with them.

4. **Stop trying to force events, people, emotions, and results.** That's your ego talking and it doesn't serve you in this situation.

5. **Find music, books, poetry, or essays that help you release your fears.** Following is a poem that a good friend of mine wrote. You can find more of his work on our Web site at www.preemieparents.com.

SLAYING DRAGONS

Slaying dragons big or small
Tis our duty to give our all
We slay dragons for the ones we love
We slay dragons to rise above
At times we slay dragons for the praise of man
And other times just to prove that we can
Sometimes we slay dragons to protect what is ours
No matter the cost no matter the hours
Yet on occasion there are dragons we just can't beat
and we find ourselves tasting defeat
often it's the same dragon we've battled for years
And it knows of our weaknesses and fears
no matter how many you've slayed in the past
this one still chases you with it's fiery blast
and though you hate it you cling to it still
it's not a battle of might but a battle of will
sometimes we face dragons that are out of our realm
and we must finally realize it's ok to hand over the helm
for during this battle this thing we call life
you must be more powerful than a sword or a knife
and be willing to ask every now and again
for help from a stranger a loved one a friend
and know that the strength we possess
will then become stronger not become less
for life is a team sport and always has been
for that is the only way we truly can win

© T. Marc 2007

S: Strength

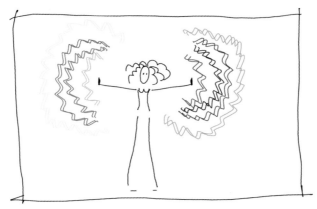

"Faith is the strength by which a shattered world shall emerge into the light." — Helen Keller

Being "strong" is a much-overused word. In fact, during my NICU journey, if one more person said to me "God doesn't give you more than you can handle" I would have screamed. I've had conversations with God about how much I can handle. I tried to throw the white flag of surrender on several occasions but it always came blowing back in my face. Apparently, the decision of what was "enough" was not mine. Nor is it yours.

As your world seems to come down around you, you must decide right away — who will be stronger, you or your circumstances? Though it may not always seem like it, your strength is a renewable resource. After a long day in the NICU when you have just enough energy to crawl into bed, tap into your faith and belief that everything is as it is supposed to be. Maintain your faith for it is the bottomless well from which you will draw your reserves. Your very belief in yourself, your baby, and the Universe keeps the flow of strength running freely through you.

Steps to Remaining Strong

1. **Lay the foundation of a strong mind.** Tell your mind that anything can happen. If your mind is ready for anything, then it will accept everything that crosses its path graciously and without much resistance.

2. **Attempt things that are seemingly beyond you,** in order to build mental strength — this could be as simple as trying a new dish in a restaurant.

3. **Mental endurance requires practice in several areas** – concentration ("B" — Being present), confidence enhancement ("Q" — Be the Queen), energy management ("R" —Releasing), anxiety reduction ("O" — Observation), and goal-setting ("U" — Understanding Intention).

4. **Exercise regularly.** Mental strength is a reflection of your physical strength.

5. **Remember that the real fight is not in the NICU,** it's in your head.

T: Trust the Power of Nature

The answer to every question you have can be found in Nature.

In a world of blood tests, X-rays, echos, ultrasounds, brain scans, body scans, and generally the most invasive medical environment imaginable, the concept of natural healing is foreign. I will acknowledge my gratitude to modern medicine and technology for they both had a huge role in saving my twins' lives. That said, long before there were hospitals, there was Nature. Before doctors, medicine men and women were the most revered members of a tribe for they could draw from the Earth's resources to heal those that they could, and give comfort to those they could not. They treated the whole person — physically, emotionally, and spiritually.

I believe that there is room for both Eastern and Western medicine as premature babies fight to survive. Allow the doctors latitude in using their methods but ask them to allow the same for you. Explore alternative remedies and therapies for everything. I used the full range of what was available to me as I supported my twins. I used flower essences and crystals to support the twins emotionally; had Reiki masters, energy healers, and medical intuitives for their spiritual well-being; and nutritional consultants and naturopathic medicine to be sure they were covered physically.

Nature is so much more than rocks, rivers, mountains, clouds, birds, trees, and flowers. The Nature that I'm referring to is beyond form. It's the energy that was here long before we were and will be here long after. We cannot separate ourselves from Nature. As we rely on traditional medicine to heal our babies, we must figure out how to invite natural medicine into the process. This will require quite a bit of advocating (refer to "A") on your part but it will be worth every minute to give your baby the best chance to excel in all aspects of his life from an early age.

Steps to Harvesting the Power of Nature

1. Get smart on natural healing before you talk to your doctors. You don't have to become an expert — just informed enough to have a dialogue with them.

2. Connect with nature on a daily basis: walk in the park, play with your pet, work in your garden. Clear your brain during these activities and see what comes to you.

3. Research has shown that patients whose rooms had a window with a view of trees had a shorter stay in the hospital. Do what you can to bring a bit of outside in to your baby.

4. Have faith. Ultimately, the human body has natural healing abilities — as a scar naturally forms over a cut. Allow the body the freedom to heal itself and it will eventually.

TAMI TIME

After nine months in the hospital, my son, Trey, was finally transferred to a rehab facility. That didn't go well and he was sent back to the hospital. He was too big for the NICU so he was sent to the Pediatric Intensive Care Unit at the hospital. The intensivists were so busy treating the symptoms and running tests that Trey's body had no time to heal. I watched him grow more despondent, as one "cured" symptom led to another problem. The antibiotics led to a fungal infection. The fungal infection resulted in gastrointestinal problems. That led to him requiring an IV. The IV became infected and he had to be put on more antibiotics. On and on this went for two months. Finally, I'd had enough and I refused to sign any more consent orders for additional procedures. I told them to take every IV out of him. Everything that he wasn't born with, that wasn't a life-saving device, I wanted out. After my first full-on temper tantrum in thirteen months, they reluctantly agreed (after making me talk to a social worker to be sure I was of sound mind, and letting me know the legalities of my decision). I started Trey on an intensive regime of nutritional supplements; I played uplifting music — not nursery rhymes — the stuff we listened to at home; and I brought his siblings to visit although it was against the rules. (I even snuck him a Popsicle® to suck on — careful with that last one.) Within hours of removing the tubes, the fever he'd had for weeks was gone. He was more alert and interactive than I'd seen him in months. The reality was that I forced the medical staff to let him heal himself. Incidentally, within ten days of taking a stand against the medical intervention, Trey was transferred successfully to the rehab facility, and from there he eventually came home.

Natural Healing Resources

HEALING WITH CRYSTALS

Crystals and gemstones are used for physical, mental, emotional, and spiritual healing. Crystals are said to direct the flow of energy to the person in a particular part of the body and bring balance to a person's energy. Ultimately, they are used to cleanse the person from bad or negative energy, which is believed to cause illness. Clearing out the bad spiritual energy alleviates the physical ailment. Not only do people visit "crystal healers," in some places, professional nurses are being trained to use crystals for their patients. I placed the crystals inside or under my twins' isolettes and continue to keep them next to their cribs.

There are hundreds of crystals available both online and at local retailers. Find someone who really understands the power of crystals to recommend an effective combination for your baby (and/or for you). I went to a small shop in my town called Little Angels. The proprietor continues to be a wealth of information about crystal healing. Over the course of my babies' stay in the NICU, she recommended the following crystals:

FOR ME:

Blue Calcite: A stone that is especially calming and soothing. Helps to calm frayed nerves. Also amplifies energy, particularly with regard to stimulating the thought process. Excellent aid to communication and fosters enlightened discussion (sounds good for dealing with doctors!).

Yellow Jasper: Quiets the nerves, encourages balance, supports you when you're under stress, protects you from and dispels negative energies, aids in quick thinking and organizational skills.

Red Jasper: Enhances confidence and understanding. Talisman for courage.

Tiger's Eye: Rebuilds feelings of self-worth (need I say more about this one?).

Pink Calcite: Calming stone that eases and heals the heart chakra. It fills the heart with universal love and self-love.

FOR THE BABIES:

Blue Calcite: In the physical realm, it is used for the throat, lungs, and respiratory system.

Yellow Jasper: For health benefits, aids with bladder and stomach problems, supports the circulatory system, and promotes the release of toxins.

Pyrite: Possesses a defending quality and is an excellent preventative that will shield one from many forms of negative energy.

Tiger's Eye: Increases personal power and heals any self-criticism. Put simply, I wanted to ensure that any issues that the twins may have had in a prior life were dealt with so they could heal more quickly in this life.

Malacite: Imparts protection, power, hope, peace, love, and success.

Pink Rose Quartz: Encourages self-love and the love of others. With so much negative stimulation, I wanted to be sure the twins knew and accepted that it was all from a place of love for them.

Rainbow Quartz: The stone of power and the master healer. It purifies and energizes all your energy bodies and activates other crystals. It absorbs radiation and protects from negative emissions. Physically, it aids with the bones, brain, radiation, strokes, soothes burns, and stimulates the immune system.

HEALING WITH FLOWER ESSENCES

Flower essences are dilute extracts of various types of flowers and plants that are used for healing. They are similar to homeopathic remedies in that they are diluted and potentized to make them more effective than just using the original flower as an herbal extract. The person who first created the original flower remedies was Dr. Edward Bach, a famous English physician. He developed the Bach Flower Remedies when he was working as a homeopathic practitioner and devoted the last years of his life to researching and developing his remedies, from 1930 onwards. The flower remedies transform inharmonious elements of the emotional and spiritual body, and lead to a gentle healing by bringing the body back in balance with itself. They act almost as a catalyst to healing.

I'd been working with Sibylle, my flower essence practitioner since early 2005 — nearly a year before my NICU experience. I'd seen firsthand the healing power of flowers in my personal and professional life. I've become more centered, balanced, and in tune with the universe. I had several sessions with Sibylle from the hospital bed to ask for her guidance and she recommended several essences for both me, my older kids, and, ultimately, the twins.

Flower essences are extremely personal. If you are interested in exploring this method of healing, visit the Web sites of flower essence companies, read the flower essence descriptions, and order according to what resonates for you. If you wish to find a local practitioner, you can do so on-line or in local holistic magazines and newspapers. As with any practitioner, it is important that you feel comfortable with the person's skill and competence, based on your own inner knowing, just as with a medical doctor. The Flower Essence Society (www.flowersociety.org) does certify practitioners.

HEALING THROUGH DIET AND NUTRITION

Your diet is the easiest thing to change to support healing. FoodNavigator-USA.com is a daily online news service available as a free-access Web site and provides daily and weekly newsletters to decision-makers in the food and beverage industry in Europe. It features great scientific and technical information about organic foods and food ingredients. www.foodnavigator-usa.com

Market America is the world's leading provider of customized nutritional supplements. They offer a wealth of information on nutrition and the science behind their products. For information on their products and more natural healing resources visit www.preemieparents.com.

U: Understanding Intention

Begin your NICU journey with the end always in mind.

Where your NICU journey will end is completely unknown to everybody. Rather than stressing over the ultimate outcome, set an intention for the future. An intention is when you stop limiting yourself to the desire for certain outcomes and you use your mind for a higher purpose. When you hold an intention for the outcome of your NICU journey, you call forth the actual awareness of the Universe and in doing so, you have at your disposal all the intelligence contained within it. You can begin doing this as you start your NICU journey by understanding the difference between thought and intention: Thought is like mailing a package to a specified address. Intention is more like being on the receiving end of a delivery, without knowing its sender or contents. With great optimism that gifts are arriving all the time, as the recipient you are only responsible for signing for the package and accepting what's inside.

Everything is energy. We are all a part of a larger flow of energy around the globe. Prior to the birth of my twins, I'd read *The Power of Intention* by

Dr. Wayne Dyer. In it, Dr. Dyer explains that intention is not something you do, it is an energy we are part of. We can access this energy to take an active role in creating the results we want in our life. If it works so well for love, happiness, finance, and health, why wouldn't it work in determining our outcome in the NICU?

My philosophy was that if I developed an intention for the twins and focused my thought on that intention as often as possible, the Universe would conspire to make my intention happen. Following is the second intention I wrote (the first being when I was on bed rest):

> We are your family and it is our intention to have you settled in our protective, loving home on or before July 4th — a day of freedom, celebration, and independence. While we await your homecoming, we bless and thank your healthcare providers for keeping you safe and nurtured in the NICU womb.
>
> Each Tuesday that passes will be a tremendous celebration of your growth, lives, and the blessings you have brought to our family.
>
> While you are here, you will be deeply nourished and encouraged to rest fully so that you can thrive and bloom into your full radiance, as a flower does. Know that wherever you are, love follows and surrounds you.
>
> So be it. And so it is.

I posted it on their bulletin board and read it when I arrived, a few times during the day, and upon leaving. My daughter, Bria, was able to come home on July 2nd; however, due to personal reasons, she actually came home on July 5th (ask me sometime about that!). My son, Trey, did not come home on or near July 4th. In fact, he spent eighteen months in a medical facility before he came home. And in doing so, he taught me a very valuable lesson about intention.

Everyone has free will and your intention cannot influence someone else's free will. While Bria was very ready to come home, Trey was not. And no amount of intending could influence that. I had to resort to living presently and changed my intention to include only those things that I could influence — my reaction to his long hospital stay, the type of mother I would be, the attitude I would have, etc.

Take a chance and set an intention for the outcome of your baby's NICU stay. Your intention for the outcome must come from a kind, loving, peaceful place. The sort of place you'd like your baby to come home to.

Steps for Tapping into the Power of Intention

1. **Don't try and figure out in your head what you should do.** Follow your heart. When you feel excessively happy, you're on to something.

2. **Take only inspired action;** that is, action that you were moved to take.

3. **To start writing your intention,** just fill in these blanks:

   a. When I arrive at the NICU each day, I want to feel
   _____.

   b. When I am visiting with my baby, I want to feel _____.

   c. When I leave the NICU each day, I want to feel _____.

4. **Start exactly where you are and start today.** Set intentions for everything you do, even the most mundane tasks. Practice makes perfect.

5. **Read *The Power of Intention* by Dr. Wayne Dyer.**

V: Victories

Celebrate every single one of your baby's milestones at a level of excitement and energy as if you'd won the biggest jackpot in the history of the lottery.

Regardless of how silly it seems, celebrate every single one of your baby's milestones big and loud and without regard for what other people think (though, as I say below, be mindful of those families who are having difficulties). My first huge celebration was when my twins survived the first night and then the first week. I remember taking a friend out for drinks when we learned that the twins' brain scans were completely normal — no blood bleeds. When the twins hit two pounds, I brought in breakfast for the nurses and doctors — I figured everyone should try and gain two pounds that morning! When Bria was extubated and put on CPAP, I took my two older kids to the park for a celebratory picnic. The first time Trey latched on and nursed, I brought him a new toy — one year later, it's still his favorite!

It's easy to go through this experience so focused on getting your baby home that you forget all of the steps in between. It is the series of little victories that gets you and them the big prize — home!

Steps to Celebrating Victories with Purpose

1. **Be sure to include everyone in the celebration** — spouse, partner, other children, the primary nurses, and attending physicians. Celebrating is uplifting for everyone in an intensive care environment.

2. **Be mindful of families who might be having difficult times.** Never cancel a celebration but be mindful of others' feelings and invite them to participate if it's appropriate.

3. **Ask the doctors and nurses what the next milestone is for your baby.** This will help you direct your thought, set your intention, and be prepared for the next celebration!

TAMI TIME

Each Tuesday marked another week in the life of my twins — both in vitro and after they were born. I celebrated every Tuesday — once a month publicly and every week by myself. It was as simple as having my favorite food for lunch on Tuesday. I never missed a Tuesday celebration and still honor each Tuesday as a blessing.

W: World: Yours Redefined

"The world seemed so large not so long ago.
But since the twins were born, it's gotten very small."
— Tami Gaines, journal entry, April 2006

I have so many friends, a relatively large family, thousands of business associates and former classmates. My circle of influence is very wide — perhaps wider than most. But somehow my world shrank a bit while I was on hospitalized bed rest for just over a month. After the twins were born, my world became very small.

The reality is that not many people can handle the intensity of the experience and the duration of the hospital stay. I had lots of support the first month or so but after that people began to drop off. Very few people are able to maintain a consistent presence in your life during this time, especially when you have limited time to speak on the phone and even less time to get together in person. At some point, people's own lives regain their attention. It seems very similar to the support someone receives when there's a death in the family. I remember when my grandfather died, my grandmother said, "I hope people don't forget to keep coming and visiting." I really understand that now.

For my part, after a long day, I was just too exhausted to recount over and over again what happened that day. I became very clear on the relationships in my life that didn't serve me or my family during this time. I was unable to engage in idle conversation, or listen to complaints or gossip because it all seemed so insignificant compared to what I was going through. Other people called every week or so and said, "Are they home yet?" "No!" I said, "And stop asking me. They'll be home when they get home." After my twentieth conversation like that, it became apparent that maintaining my relationships in any way I could would have to be good enough until I got through this. Those who felt put off or ignored probably weren't as close to me as I'd thought.

There were others who I hadn't spoken with in years and they just showed up. My friends from Columbia Business School, Eddie and Karen, had also had a preemie with significant medical challenges. We hadn't talked in a year or more. One very late night, I arrived home to find the refrigerator stocked full of food — every shelf was jam-packed with the most delicious, homemade food that one could imagine. It was all prepared in labeled containers. I was totally confused until I found a note on the counter: "Just stopped by to see if we could help." They had no idea…or perhaps they did. It still brings tears to my eyes because I didn't even know that they were in my small world. As Haili and Shane told me of these unknown visitors that came by, it was like they were retelling of the gifts they received on Christmas.

At first, having a smaller world was very isolating. Every now and again, someone would pop up to remind me that there are seasons for people. It was a waste of time for me to pine over the seeming loss of relationships or grow frustrated at my inability to make time to maintain them. I was grateful for those who were still there and I accepted, once again, that everything happens for a reason. And I found peace in my new, smaller world.

Steps to Redefining Your World

1. Remember that your journey in the NICU is just a point in time. You will not be in this place forever and there will be time to rekindle relationships if that's what is in your greatest good.

2. Redefining your world is not something you do consciously. It happens over time. People drop out and others step in. Most didn't understand the medical implications of all that the twins had gone through but they appreciated the emotional roller coaster I was living. The community of people that hung in there from the very beginning consisted of friends, family, and fans who will be with me until the end of time no matter what the circumstance.

3. One of the hidden benefits of the NICU experience is a weeding out of your relationship garden. The weakest plants that might not have made it anyway, die off. The weeds that might have otherwise taken over, are picked clean. All that remains are the strongest, healthiest, most beautiful flowers for you to appreciate and enjoy.

continued on next page...

TAMI TIME

I recently ran into a friend. The last time I talked to him was literally from the hospital bed while on bed rest. It had been almost a year and a half. We hugged and when we pulled back, he had tears streaming down his face. "What did I do to make you cut me off like that? I can't understand what happened between us." My first reaction was to laugh, "Mark, since the last time we spoke, my husband left, I had premature twins, and a host of other things that you couldn't possibly imagine have happened. Trust me, the sun does not rise and set on you!" He laughed, too. Your incredibly shrinking world is not without consequences.

4. By the way, speaking of redefining, there are a few hidden jewels of the NICU that most dare not speak of! Sssshhhhh... here are a few:

Sleep – You: It might be fitful but at least you're getting some. That wouldn't happen if your baby was home!

Sleep – Them: There's no need to rock them, sing to them, walk them around the house for hours on end, or drive them around the block — unless you want to. NICU babies put themselves to sleep and they usually stay that way!

Newborn Schedule: Most new parents are trying to get their babies on a schedule so they can manage their lives. Your baby comes home with the schedule handed to you on paper.

Noise: Did you ever go to a friend's house and it's like a library all the time so the baby can sleep? Your NICU baby can sleep through ANYTHING. Just try vacuuming under his crib and you'll see what I mean.

The Dream Team: Under what other circumstance could you have a Dream Team of medical specialists at your beck and call daily to talk to you about nothing but your baby's health?

Babysitter/Stranger Anxiety: They've been taken care of by a rotation of strangers in the NICU. What's another new face to them?

If you'd like to add to this list and bring a bit of humor to preemie parents everywhere, visit our Web site – www.preemieparents.com.

X: Examine Your Priorities

*Henry David Thoreau said, "It's not enough to be busy;
so are the ants. The question is what are we busy about?"
Whatever you are busy about pales by comparison to the focus
and energy this NICU journey will require. Let it all go.
It will be there when you return.*

B efore my hospitalized bed rest and before the twins were born, I was a woman on fire — always running, going, dropping off, picking up, volunteering — being Superwoman was my full-time job and I have the shadow of the "S" on my chest to prove it. It's only a shadow at this point because once I discovered that I was pregnant — and a high-risk, twin pregnancy at that — I had to hang up my cape and focus on only the most important things in my life: My children, both born and unborn.

Once I committed to the health of my twins and remaining healthy at all costs, it became very easy to walk away from so many of the things that consumed me. At the end of the day, none of it mattered — PTA meetings, block parties, board meetings, consulting projects, weekends away. I realized that they'd all be there when I made it through this journey. And if they weren't, all the better!

You must learn to discriminate among all of the things you HAVE to get done: work, the laundry, birthday parties, etc. They cannot all be of equal importance. When all is said and done, nothing is more important than the health and wellness of your children. Learn to let go (see "R"), be present (see "B"), and trust that you are exactly where you're supposed to be right now.

Steps to Examine Your Priorities

1. **Things have to get done.** After all, life must go on. Be careful not to create impossible situations for yourself. Review every obligation to determine how realistic it is given your situation.

2. **Stress can lead to sickness and you cannot afford to be sick right now.** If part of your stress is a result of being overcommitted, decide right now what you will walk away from, even if it's only temporarily. And then walk.

3. **Make a "big" list of everything that must get done at the start of each week.** Immediately cross off everything that can wait a few weeks or months! Circle anything that you can delegate to a willing family member and quickly call them to do it. Review the remaining items and choose one or two to do each day.

4. **Remember, it can't all be that important.**

Y: Don't Ask "Why" Unless You Are Advocating

Accepting your situation for what it is is the first step in your NICU journey. Refusing to ask "why?" is at the end of this book because it's graduation. When you can just be in this experience, without question, you've made it.

I can remember back to the day in the hospital when, during my routine ultrasound, it was revealed that I was in full labor. As I sat alone watching the fetal monitor, all I could think was:

"Why did this happen to me?"

"What did I do wrong?"

"Why is God punishing me?"

Being on bed rest, ripped out of my life, and forced to be on the outside looking in, I understood that it didn't matter why. The answer to that question wouldn't change any of the events that had happened or were going to happen. Asking why will not produce any significant information to you. In fact, no one can answer that question for you. The "why" will be revealed in the lessons you learn on the journey.

A far better question is "What am I to learn from this?" Ask yourself that, whether something goes wrong or right. This book is full of answers to that question, asked over and over again from my very long NICU journey.

REPLACE THE "WHY?" WITH THE "WHAT?" TO LEARN THE LESSONS THAT LIFE IS TEACHING YOU.

Z: Zero In: Focus

*It is so easy to become distracted in the NICU,
to get caught up in bells, alarms, test results, other families'
problems, the doctors you love, and the nurses you don't.
There is so much to deal with on a daily basis that losing sight
of the finish line is almost inevitable. But in order to get
where you're going, you must be able to see it clearly.*

We've covered a lot of ground in this book and it pales in comparison to the amount of information you are getting and will get during your NICU journey. You'll see things you should never have seen and have conversations that you'd never have imagined. You'll be forced to make life and death decisions. You'll lose friends and gain new ones. You'll curse at the gas station attendant and cry to the babysitter. It's just so much to handle and so unbelievable. But it is real and it is happening to you right now.

I encourage you to zero in on the ultimate goal — to get your baby out of the NICU. Regardless of what happens during the course of the day, focus, focus, focus. As long as you are stepping on the path toward home, even if gingerly, it will all be all right. Even if you've been forward and back and round and round on the same path toward home, focus on home.

If it is destined to be, your baby will be home with you one day. You will hold your baby in your arms and rock him to sleep in the quiet serenity of your home. You will be able to show her off without visitation restrictions. You will see him hit so many more milestones in his life. This is just a point in time and you will not be here forever.

thoughts from the cribside

You may never have more time to just sit and think than during your NICU journey. My thoughts wandered from here to there — from imagining owning a glorious house on a beach to wondering how I'd look in the dress the mom next to me was wearing. All of that downtime is a thought garden — sprouting ideas, musings, and imagined concerns about the future. My journey became more scary as I got closer to the discharge of my daughter. After nearly four months in the hospital, Bria was doing great and the day would soon come when they told me I could take her home. My anxiety over her homecoming was surprising and powerful. Here's a few thoughts for you as you near the end of your NICU journey.

ON THE PATH HOME...

As my daughter grew stronger and stronger, I finally asked her primary nurse for her plans to get Bria home. At that point, Bria was still on oxygen support and was nippling a few feeds a day. Her nurse looked me in the eye and said, "We have a choice to make. A hard one. We can either focus on feeding or breathing but not both." "But she needs both to live," I protested. "But she only needs to conquer one to go home. The other can be dealt with." I chose feeding. We focused on getting Bria to take all of her feeds from a bottle or from the breast. When she successfully did that, they discharged her. I took her home on oxygen. One day, she wouldn't need the oxygen anymore. And all of the days between her discharge and that day when she is free of the nasal canula are days she spent at home with our family. She came home sooner because we agreed to focus on either feeding or breathing but not both. Everything is a tradeoff in the NICU. Everything.

ON GOING HOME...

Like all else, the news of your discharge is unexpected, scary, and will bring up a wave of different emotions. It was bound to happen. You just spent so much time "being present" that you did not see it coming!

Congratulations. You won the war. Even though your baby might be going home with certain equipment, be sure not to take the hospital home with you. Leave the stress, uncertainty, critical care nursery habits, and worry in the NICU. Take with you the confidence that the doctors would never discharge a baby that wasn't ready; they'd never discharge a baby whose caregivers weren't ready; they'd never discharge a baby that needed to take the hospital home with them. Take all of that with you. And don't forget to take your baby.

ON PARENTING A NICU BABY...

Once you're finally home, everyone wants to celebrate the miracle baby. You are constantly reminded of the NICU journey and the pain of it all is still fresh in your heart. You bring your baby home and treat her with kid gloves, afraid of infection, apnea, readmittance to the hospital. Perhaps you had to come home with medical equipment and are constantly running back and forth to the doctor. At some point, your premature baby must become just your baby. Eventually, you have to let go of what she *was* and treat her as she *is* so that she can become who she is *meant to be*.

ON THE DEATH OF A BABY...

There is another reality that I was faced with every single day of my NICU journey — the death of my baby. While Bria was very sick and medically fragile at birth, I watched her get stronger and stronger and hit her growth benchmarks consistently. After a period of time, she had very few setbacks and I knew with confidence that she'd come home.

Trey, on the other hand, was an entirely different story. He died in my arms dozens of times. I often came in the morning and they were bagging him to bring him back to life. I got THE CALL several times to come and see Trey because they didn't think he was going to make it through the night. I never focused on the possibility of losing him but nevertheless, it was an ongoing reality for the first sixteen months of his life.

Trey did make it; however, I was witness to many other babies who did not. I gave support and condolences to the parents and caregivers who lost their babies. In fact, when the twins were first admitted to the NICU, the neighboring babies on each side of them passed. I don't remember exactly what I said to their parents in that moment or even at the wake that I attended. I do know that I would tell those babies the following:

God lent you to us — an angel to show us the light of love, hope, and possibility. Most people spend a lifetime searching for what you gave us in just a few hours, days, weeks, or months. With no fear, you give us one last look as if to say, "It's right." And then God encircled you in His arms and you left a bit of heaven in each of us. Today, I learned that it is possible to be in grief and joy at the same time.

closing thoughts

Ultimately, this is a story of strength when weakness makes the most sense. Of tuning in when being oblivious is the easiest path. Of advocating without the confidence to do so. Of being the person your baby will be proud of long after this is over. Of having faith in the divine plan rather than anger at your situation. Of using the healing power of thought to gain strength, confidence, and the faith that this is just a point in time and when you leave this place, you will never be the same again.

I was trying to conceive of the perfect ending for this book and then I realized that there is none. Our story is still being written. None of us are the same characters we were in the beginning of the story. We have all evolved and been elevated to an entirely different status here on this earth. I have been given four earth angels and I've become a messenger and a conduit through which the Universe works. I will do whatever is asked without question — passionately and with joy.

When I first wrote *Preemie Parents*, it was sixteen months after our NICU journey first began and it had yet to end. It's now been four years. In the end, Bria stayed in the NICU for four months. She came home on oxygen, on many medications, and with several monitors. Within a year, she no longer needed oxygen and monitors and we weaned her off of the prescriptions.

Trey had a much more difficult journey. He spent nine months in the NICU, followed immediately by four months in the pediatric intensive care unit, after which he was discharged to a rehabilitation hospital, where he stayed for almost five months. It was a fight to get him home — the insurance company wanted to institutionalize him. When Trey finally came home, he did so with a trach, on a ventilator, on oxygen, eating through a gastrostomy tube ("G-Tube"), and on dozens of medications. For more than a year after he came home, Trey was in and out of the hospital regularly and we made many, many calls to 911. Today, Trey is being weaned off of his ventilator and oxygen. He's down to just four prescriptions and, although he's still primarily eating through a g-tube, he's learning to eat from a spoon. For a child who was not supposed to make it out of the NICU, he's doing phenomenally well. I'm so proud of both Bria and Trey.

We dodged many bullets and we feel very blessed. We did not move through our journey unscathed; however, we have wounds that have healed into scars. Eventually, they will disappear and we will become whole again.

I survived my twins' journey by identifying and learning the lessons presented to me. I focused on opportunities for personal growth and celebrated every small success the babies achieved. I did not dwell on the past and did not look too far into the future. I blessed the healthcare providers every day and showed gratitude for everyone and everything, including the experience of the NICU.

Just last year, I decided that the twins needed their own bedroom and I planned on making one out of the attic. The thought was daunting since there were thirteen years of furniture, boxes, bags of old clothes, and all sorts of junk up there. But I had a vision for what that room could be. My older son was helping me clean out the garbage. He was laughing because I wasn't even opening boxes. I was just dragging them to the curb. "What if you need something in there?" he asked me. I told him that if it hadn't been needed, searched for, and wanted in the last decade, whatever was in there was trash and we just needed to take it out — to make a speedy decision so we could get to the finish line. He thought about that and we worked in silence.

An hour later, we had a huge pile of garbage at the curb. We went back upstairs and sat smiling at our handiwork — a completely clean space that we could make into anything we wanted. Shane startled me when he said, "I'm so proud of you, Mom." I grinned at the thought of whatever could come next from the mouth of this wise nine-year-old. "Why?" I asked, waiting for the joke.

"Because after Dad left, I was so sad and angry for such a long time. And then the twins were in the hospital and Trey kept going to the hospital after he came home. I thought everything was going to fall apart. I thought you were going to go away…not really your body but your mind…I thought you couldn't handle everything. It's why I didn't smile for so long. But look at what you did. The house is still standing and it's better than it was when Dad was here. We're all so happy. We have people over all the time and it feels like everything is a big party. Every day is a fun day. Even this," he waved his arms around, "you just decided to make a bedroom up here and then you did what you had to do make that happen. Next week, we'll have a bedroom. That's really cool. So are you."

It's been just over four years since all of this started. It took a quick conversation in an empty attic with my son, for me to acknowledge all that I'd accomplished; to honor the pillar that I'd become for my kids; and to embrace the fact that we're still going through it. But I have the tools to navigate whatever comes and the realistic perspective that things will always come.

And now you do, too. I'll leave you with this final thought:

**BE WHERE YOU ARE
BUT
SEE WHERE YOU'RE GOING.**

resources

Web sites for Medical Information

The following Web sites provide information on the care and concerns associated with prematurity. These are Web sites developed by and for government, health, and advocacy organizations. The information is credible and provides a good starting point for online research.

WebMD: www.webmd.com

Medline Plus: www.nlm.nih.gov/medlineplus/prematurebabies.html

American Academy of Family Physicians: http://familydoctor.org/online/famdocen/home/children/parents/infants/283.html

Healthline: www.healthline.com

Science Daily: www.sciencedaily.com

March of Dimes: www.marchofdimes.com/prematurity

American Academy of Pediatrics: www.aap.org

National Institute of Child Health & Human Development: www.nichd.nih.gov

Nutritional Supplement Regime

There are literally hundreds of nutritional supplements on the market today and they are not all created equally. Having had some nutrition training, I use supplements that are in isotonic form because they have the best absorption into the body based on clinical evidence. More detailed information on each of the regimes below can be found online at www.preemieparents.com.

Daily Supplements for Maintaining Optimum Health

OPC-3: A super antioxidant used to fight free radical damage, which is caused when we do anything unnatural to our bodies. Sitting in a room surrounded by machines, breathing recirculated air, and being in a state of constant stress is all very unnatural.

Prenatal Multivitamin: Good for any woman with health issues, blood disorders, and chronic diseases, as well as vegetarians, vegans, women with prior pregnancy complications, women with lactose intolerance, and smokers. It also has more iron, calcium, folic acid, vitamins, and minerals for recovery and it helps increase maternal nutrient stores. I decided to stay on the prenatal multivitamin because of the beating my body took.

Vitamin B-Complex: Positively impacts blood cells, stress, seratonin levels, and the nervous system — to help keep you calm and relaxed. It's also great for energy.

Vitamin D & Calcium: The majority of the population is deficient in Vitamin D, a supplement that's excellent for the body's immune system. Without Vitamin D, your body has difficulty absorbing calcium. In the case of your preemie journey, calcium provides great relief for insomnia.

Other Supplements

At certain points, I added nutritional supplements for specific incidents. Certainly, in the beginning of the journey, I was under constant stress — chronic stress, if you will. In addition to the optimum health regime noted above, I added Bliss™ Anti-Stress Formula, which promotes relaxation without drowsiness, helps stabilize your mood, and is ideal for any individual encountering consistently stressful days or an upcoming stressful event.

The science behind these products and more information can be found at www.preemieparents.com.

Exercise Regime

I had several friends who were exercise physiologists and personal trainers. I asked them for exercises that I could do while sitting in the NICU, both for the energy boost and to stave off boredom! Here are some exercises that they gave me:

Marching (start at 5 minutes and then build from there)

- Start by sitting straight up in the chair with head and shoulders back and your feet planted squarely on the floor.

- Lift your right foot off the floor in marching fashion and then do the same with your left foot – right, left, right, left.

- **Key Point:** Put your foot down rather than letting it drop to the floor.

Thigh Squeezes (start at 12 squeezes per leg and work up from there)

- Place a pillow between your knees and squeeze your thighs together.

- Hold for 5 seconds and relax. This strengthens your inner thighs.

- To work on the outer thighs, remove the pillow and place your hands on the outside of each thigh. Push against them. Again, hold for 5 seconds and relax.

Heel Raises (start at 12 raises per leg and work up from there)

- Start with your feet flat on the ground.

- Lift your heels up until you go up on your toes.

- Slowly bring your feet back down to the ground. This helps to strengthen your calf muscles in your lower legs.

Toe Raises (start at 12 raises per leg and work up from there)

- Start with your feet flat on the ground.

- This time, lift your toes off the floor and point them to the ceiling.

- Relax and lower them to the floor.

Knee Extensions *(start at 12 extensions per leg and work up from there)*

- Sit upright in a chair.

- Raise your lower leg until it is straight (horizontal).

- Slowly lower the leg all the way to the floor.

- Repeat with the other leg.

Abdominal Vacuum *(for flatter abs — start at 12 breaths and work up from there)*

- Sit upright in a chair.

- Start by exhaling absolutely every bit of air from your lungs.

- Pull the navel towards the spine as if I just told you to suck in your stomach.

- Continue to breathe lightly through your nostrils, but make sure you're pulling your navel in as tight as possible.

- **Key Point:** You must hold the contraction very tight for at least 40 seconds.

Water bottle alternating front-shoulder raise *(start at 12 and work up from there)*

- Sit straight with your knees slightly bent and feet shoulder-width apart.

- Hold a water bottle in your right hand with your arm in front of you and your palms lightly resting on your thighs.

- Contracting the front shoulder muscles, lift your right arm in front of you until it is slightly above shoulder-height.

- Slowly return the right arm to the starting position.

- After completing 12-15 reps on the right side, switch to the left.

Water bottle biceps curl *(start at 12 and work up from there)*

- Sit upright, feet forward and your head a natural extension of your spine.

- Hold a water bottle in your right hand with your arms hanging down at your sides and palms facing your body.

- Keep your wrists straight throughout the exercise.

- Contracting the biceps muscles, bend your right arm at the elbow while turning your wrist until your palm is just short of touching your shoulder.

- Slowly return to the starting position, stopping just short of the elbow, fully extending the arm.

- After 12-15 repetitions, repeat on the other side.

- **Key points:** Your upper arm should remain stationary throughout the exercise.

One-arm tricep kickback *(start at 12 and work up from there)*

- While seated, bend forward very slightly.

- Hold a water bottle in your right hand or just make a fist. Bend the elbow at a 90-degree angle, pointing behind you with the upper arm not quite parallel to the floor.

- Contracting your triceps muscles, move your lower arm back until the bottle or fist is pointing away from your body to the rear of the room.

- Slowly return to the starting position.

- After completing the set on the right side, repeat on the left side.

- **Key point:** Your upper arm should remain stationary throughout the exercise.

Financial Freedom

The conversation around money and achieving financial freedom is one that is bigger and longer than the scope of this book. This is just a starting point and I encourage you to get started!

Knowing that one of the biggest keys to wealth is changing your mindset, the following is a list of books that I recommend to help get you started.

Recommended Reading

- *The Secrets of the Millionaire Mind,* T. Harv Eker
- *The One-Minute Millionaire,* Mark Victor Hansen and Robert Allen
- *Rich Dad's Retire Young, Retire Rich,* Robert T. Kiyosaki and Sharon Lechter
- *Rich Dad, Poor Dad,* Robert T. Kiyosaki and Sharon Lechter
- *The Alchemist,* Paulo Coelho
- *The Way to Wealth,* Benjamin Franklin
- *Seven Spiritual Laws of Success,* Deepak Chopra
- *As A Man Thinketh*, James Allen
- *The Strangest Secret*, Earl Nightingale
- *The Richest Man in Babylon*, George S. Clason
- *Think & Grow Rich,* Napoleon Hill

The following wealth principles come from *The Secrets of the Millionaire Mind: Mastering the Inner Game of Wealth.* This list represents ten of the dozens that are offered in the book and are particularly relevant to your journey of prematurity.

Fundamental Principles of Wealth Creation

1. Your income can only grow to the extent that you do!

2. Money is a result, wealth is a result, health is a result, illness is a result, your weight is a result. We live in a world of cause and effect.

3. Thoughts lead to feelings. Feelings lead to actions. Actions lead to results.

4. When the subconscious mind must choose between deeply rooted emotions and logic, emotions will almost always win.

5. The only way to change the temperature in the room is to reset the thermostat. In the same way, the only way to change your level of financial success "permanently" is to reset your financial thermostat.

6. Consciousness is observing your thoughts and actions so that you can live from true choices in the present moment rather than being run by programming from the past.

7. Money is extremely important in the areas in which it works, and extremely unimportant in the areas in which it doesn't.

8. There is no such thing as a really rich victim!

9. The number one reason most people don't get what they want is that they don't know what they want.

10. If you are not fully, totally, and truly committed to creating wealth, chances are you won't.

Passive Income

Passive income is an area that confuses most people. Passive income generally comes from a business or an activity that you do once and it pays you for a very long time on that one effort. Passive income is money working for you, not you working for it and generally, we are referring to *passive business income.* Everyone should own their own business, for tax reasons and because your boss will NEVER let you make more than they do!

Here are some ideas for passive business income — businesses that you build once and they pay you forever:

- Storage Units
- Parking Lots
- Vending Machines
- Laundromats
- ATMs
- Car Washes
- Campgrounds
- DVD Vending Machines
- Franchising

My favorite of all the businesses that you can start with little capital investment and potentially huge returns are network marketing businesses. Network marketing began in the 1950s and is often misunderstood by those who don't understand the power of the industry. The easiest way to explain what this industry is at its core is to give you a scenario. What was the last great movie you saw? When the movie was over, did you go home and tell someone about it? When you told them, did they go see the movie? If they did, did the movie studio send you a check for referring your friend to the movie? Of course not! But that scenario is essentially what happens in the network marketing industry. There are companies that exist that will pay you for spreading positive information about their products and services. If people purchase, you get paid — either profit, commission, or both. What's so great about that? If you're the parent of a premature baby, there are many pluses:

- You work from home.

- You make your own hours.

- You are your own boss so there's no one to answer to when you need to be present in the NICU, or upon discharge, when you need take your baby to a doctor's appointment.

- You become a business owner and get many tax write-offs because of that.

- You can make a significant part-time income, replace your current income, or become a professional and earn full-time income and more!

The industry is flooded with companies and, often, to the untrained person, it is very difficult to tell one apart from another. When I first explored this industry, I wanted to be home with my kids, work on my own terms, and create a six-figure income — remember financial freedom?! With an MBA from Columbia University, I have access to some of the best business minds on the planet. In an effort to understand how to evaluate a company, I spoke with a very senior manager at American Express, with significant experience in the networking industry. He told me four things to look for in a network marketing company:

1. Find a company with high-quality products, on the leading edge of their industry, that sell themselves because most people aren't natural salespeople.

2. Find a company with people who you trust and respect.

3. Find a company with a phenomenal training system (since I'd never done this before).

4. Find a company with a business and compensation plan that the average person can follow to success without making an extraordinary effort — 80 percent of the world is average!

After much exploration, I settled on a phenomenal company that surpassed the criteria laid out above. It's been eight years since I began working with them and the experience has far exceeded my expectations. With each passing year, I've gotten better at my business, have grown personally, and have created more income, for myself and others, than I originally thought possible. It's because of my relationship with this company that I was able to spend eighteen months in the hospital with my twins.

By the way, during those eighteen months, I all but stopped building my business. I simply didn't have the mental space to manage it with everything else I had going on. Although I stopped working, my income did not stop. I received the same commission check every single week. Passive business income is one of the most important keys to your financial freedom.

More information on this topic can be found at www.preemieparents.com

Soul Boosters

20 WAYS TO REVIVE YOUR HEART AND SOUL

One of the ways to successfully navigate your NICU experience is by having an unlimited supply of energy. You'll need to able to draw on your energy pool at any time of the day or night to keep your spirits high, your attention on the most important things, and to generally live the *Preemie Parents* principles. Here are 20 proven ways to increase your energy — spiritually, mentally, and physically.

1. Eat a balanced, low-glycemic (low-sugar content) diet that consists of raw fruits and vegetables, nuts (like almonds and cashews), whole grains (not white bread) and fish (especially halibut). Most of all, remember to eat!

2. Get moving! Did you know that a brisk ten-minute walk will increase your energy and that that energy will last for up to two hours. Walk around the NICU, the parking lot, or even to the cafeteria to get some great food.

3. Take a power nap. Research has shown that pushing our brains too hard can take a lot of energy. The National Institute of Mental Health found that a sixty-minute "power nap" can help reverse the mind-numbing effects of information overload and stress.

4. Do whatever you can to reduce stress.

5. Drink less alcohol and more water. I love wine. In fact, it's one of my few vices — a glass of fantastic wine at the end of the day is always a perfect ending — no matter what sort of day I've had. I realized very quickly, though, that I'd need to reduce my wine intake and increase my water intake if I was to conserve my energy.

6. Breathe deeply. Here's how to do this in the NICU:

   A. Sit or stand upright with your head and back supported.

   B. Place your hand on your abdomen, just under your belly button.

C. Inhale deeply through your nose while gently pushing out your belly. You should feel your hand on your belly moving outward.

D. Exhale slowly using pursed lips, while gently pushing inward and upward on your belly with your hand to help empty your lungs completely.

E. Practice this breathing technique until you are comfortable doing it anywhere, at any time.

7. Get off the coffee! Although coffee gives you an initial pop of energy, it can promote burnout. Gradually cut back to one cup per day. There are many great coffee substitutes. My favorite is a product called Mochatonix™. It gives you energy and promotes weight loss — that's a bonus! You can find more details on Mochatonix™ at www.preemieparents.com.

8. Review my nutritional supplement routine on pages 125-126. This combination enabled me to maintain optimum health under stress and increase energy.

9. Take twenty minutes every day for yourself. Whether reading a book, listening to music, meditating, or just sitting, these twenty minutes will get you farther than almost anything.

10. Remember "V" victories? Celebrate all wins in the NICU! The simple act of clapping and cheering changes your state of mind.

11. Focus on the positive. Being a pessimist takes a lot of energy.

12. Go home and take a shower. It will wake up your brain and your body.

13. Give into one of your cravings and indulge yourself.

14. Get a massage. That's a great energy booster!

15. Use aromatherapy. Peppermint, ginger, and citrus smells boost energy.

16. Listen to some music that is heart-pumping and makes you want to dance.

17. Avoid people who sap your energy.

18. Review all that you accomplished each day. The act of celebrating your own successes will give you massive energy.

19. Help someone or volunteer. Being of service to others gives an instant energy boost. On one of Trey's "bad" days, I went to the hospital cafeteria to get some hot chocolate. As my turn came at the cashier, she said, "Will that be all?" "No, I'll take care of this lady's coffee too," I said, turning to the woman behind me. She accepted graciously and I felt much better, as I headed back to the NICU.

20. As difficult as it may be at times, you must get on a regular sleep schedule. When you do sleep, be sure that you're getting a great night's sleep, even if it's for just a few hours. Be sure to sleep in a fully darkened bedroom (turn your alarm clock away from you if the display gives off too much light and turn the TV off). Your bedroom should be moderately cool (you'll wake up if it's too hot or too cold) and using white noise (a fan or quiet music) will help induce sleepiness.

glossary

Apnea: When a baby stops breathing for more than twenty seconds, or if his heart rate or color changes during the breathing lapse, then it is called apnea.

Bradycardia: Typically as a result of apnea, bradycardia is when the baby's heart rate drops to a rate of less than 100 beats per minute (rather than the usual range of 120-160 beats).

CPAP: When a baby does not need a lot of help from a respirator but is not quite ready to breathe on her own, she will have prongs inserted in her nose that will give her a steady flow of air.

Desat: When the oxygen in the blood falls below acceptable levels.

Echocardiograph: A diagnostic test that uses ultrasound waves to create an image of the heart muscle.

Extubate: Removing the tube from your baby's nose, as he is taken off the ventilator.

G-Tube (Gastrostomy Tube): A tube placed directly into the stomach to feed a baby rather than feeding by mouth.

Intubate: When the tube is put into your baby's nose so she can be on the ventilator.

IVH: IVH is short for "intraventricular hemorrhage." IVH is bleeding inside or around the spaces in the brain containing the cerebral spinal fluid. Intraventricular hemorrhage is most common in premature babies, especially very low-birthweight babies weighing less than 1,500 grams (3 pounds, 5 ounces). Bleeding can occur because blood vessels in a premature baby's brain are very fragile and immature and can easily rupture. The smaller and more premature the baby, the more likely IVH will occur. Nearly all IVH occurs within the first three days of life. Bleeding in the brain can put pressure on the nerve cells and damage them. Severe damage to cells can lead to brain injury.

Magnesium: Magnesium Sulfate is a commonly used drug for treating preterm labor. It is given intravenously and slows contractions, although the effect and how long it lasts varies from woman to woman. Studies have shown that magnesium sulfate can delay delivery for at least several days (depending on how far dilated a woman's cervix is when the medication is started). This isn't a lot of time, but it can make a big difference for the fetus. Doctors do not know exactly how magnesium sulfate inhibits contractions. The most common explanation is that magnesium lowers calcium levels in uterine muscle cells. Since calcium is necessary for muscle cells to contract, this is thought to relax the uterine muscle.

PDA: A blood vessel near the heart that normally closes within ten days of birth. In 25 percent of premature babies, it does not close. When it is open, it causes too much blood flow through the lungs, making respiratory issues worse.

Phototherapy: In *Preemie Parents,* I refer to "sunlights." This is called phototherapy and it is used to treat jaundice in premature babies that is caused by issues with the liver. In this condition, the liver, which helps filter waste products from the blood, cannot rid the body of bilirubin, a substance produced during the normal breakdown of red blood cells. As a result, bilirubin accumulates in the baby's blood and spreads into the tissues. Because bilirubin is a yellowish color, the baby's skin takes on a yellowish tint. Phototherapy — which involves placing a baby under bright lights — is the standard treatment for jaundice. During treatment, the baby's eyes are covered with eye patches to protect him from glare. The baby is turned from front to back, or lights are used both overhead and underneath the baby, so that all of the skin is exposed to the light. The light helps break down the bilirubin into a substance that the body can excrete more easily. Usually phototherapy is needed for about a week, and after that, the liver is mature enough to excrete bilirubin on its own.

Pulmonary Hypertension: A common disorder of prematurity characterized by increased blood pressure in the lungs.

Tracheostomy: A surgical procedure during which a tube is inserted into the trachea and then is connected to a ventilator.

Ventilator: A ventilator is a breathing machine that mechanically assists patients in the exchange of oxygen and carbon dioxide (sometimes referred to as artificial respiration).

preemie parents foundation

I am passionate about helping parents of premature babies grow through their NICU experience. I always believed that my commitment was to be more than a book. In 2008, I founded The Preemie Parents Foundation, a 501(c)3-pending organization to meet the needs of preemie parents everywhere.

On August 25, 2009, the *New York Times* reported on post-traumatic stress disorder suffered by parents of babies in the NICU. Both Duke University and Stanford University released reports that say parents of NICU infants experience multiple traumas that are termed "post-traumatic stress disorder," the effects of which could last for years. Post-traumatic stress is most often associated with "surviving war, car accidents, and assault."

While numerous financial and medical resources are available for the premature baby, few exist to support the families as they move through this experience. The families and caregivers of these babies are unexpectedly launched into an emotional, physical, and spiritual roller coaster with little guidance to help them navigate the scary, unpredictable world of ringing emergency bells and medical chaos. The emotional, financial, and physical stress placed on these families is unimaginable. *The Preemie Parents Foundation provides services and support that ensure that the parents will survive, even if their baby doesn't.*

Our mission is to provide the parents and caregivers of premature babies with the tools, resources, and support needed to transform this unexpected journey from a place of bewilderment to one of empowerment.

Please visit our Web site to learn more about the organization, our programs and services, and how you can support it. We're also compiling a list of preemie parents so we can create a powerful online community. Please be sure to register on the Web site — www.preemieparentsfoundation.org. Thank you!

Index